The Survivalists

THE SURVIVALISTS

Patrick Rivers

Universe Books
New York

Published in the United States of America in 1976 by
Universe Books, 381 Park Avenue South, New York,
N.Y. 10016.

© 1975 Patrick Rivers

Library of Congress Catalog Card Number: 75-33484

Cloth edition: ISBN 0-87663-272-X
Paperback edition: ISBN 0-87663-931-7

Printed in the United States of America.

Contents

Acknowledgements

In the making of the journey and the writing of the book, too many people helped me for me to acknowledge every one. However, for the help they extended – whether hospitality, transport, enlightenment, encouragement or criticism – I should like to thank Steve Boulter, Robin Clarke, John Davoll, Harold Dickinson, Anne Donner, Peter van Dresser, Peter Harper, Herbert L. Hiller, Steve Kaffka, Ethel Mannin, Dammy and John Manson, Jack Parsons, Kit Pedler, Richard Merrill, Sim van der Ryn, John Seymour, John Shore, John Shuttleworth, Sally and Philip Toynbee, Elizabeth and H. F. Wallis, Steve Weichart, Stan Windass, and Terry Winnington, and the people at Eithin y Gaer, Integrated Life Support Systems, Laurieston Hall, the Life Centre, New Alchemy Institute, Project One and Village Design.

That I have acknowledged these people and groups does not, of course, mean that they necessarily agree with views expressed in the book; nor does my wife, Shirley, who typed its many drafts and bore the ensuing adversity bravely – though I suspect she would not have continued the journey if she were not in accord with most of them.

Prologue

At some point in my life – I shall never know when – I discovered that society was sick. At first I was naïve enough to think that my diagnosis was original, but I soon found that I was not alone in thinking the way I did. This comforted me for it meant that perhaps I was not mad after all.

Many people, I learned, shared my belief, but felt powerless to do anything about it. Others had broken the inertia barrier and, as I encountered more people who were thinking seriously about this not inconsequential problem, I was struck by a number of things about them. They belonged, it seemed, to The Alternative, but they were not all young and stoned, and it was not strictly necessary to grow a beard and eat brown rice to feel at ease with them. More significantly they offered hope in what had seemed a hopeless situation. While differing on politics, philosophy and strategy, they all agreed that it was too late to 'patch up' the kind of society we have; we must find a fairer, more enjoyable one that will last, and we must find it quickly. (The society we now have, by the way, is seen as terminal.)

Outnumbered, weak and divided they might be, but my new fellow travellers were the nucleus of an alternative society. In time I began to feel part of it and I knew there was no turning back; for as one of them put it: 'When you have seen the vision, you have the responsibility.' Helped at all times by my wife who shared the vision, I took a few steps to move outside of 'straight' society and then travelled several thousand miles to write this book – a journey which was to be no more than the beginning of a far longer one of a different kind.

I am told that this is a potentially dangerous, subversive book, for if the ideas which it unfolds were to take hold they would bring down the system! We shall see. Some people who 'have the vision' are compelled to take drastic action; others feel they can better achieve the necessary change by staying where they are – even though they may feel they no longer belong there.

This book seeks to acquaint people who are still 'inside the system' with the nature of that part of the alternative society which recognises the importance of awareness and action – people who have felt constrained to *do* rather than talk about what should be done. This is not another 'theory' book, nor will it give details on how to build a methane digester. Instead it concentrates on telling how various people came to change their views and ways, and at times it also attempts to assess the relevance of what they are trying to do.

The beginning of the first chapter plunges straight into describing some of these 'survivalists', as I have called them, and we encounter others throughout the book. At first they may seem a disparate minority but as we get to know them better, they turn out to have much in common.

As you read on, you may find that you too have more in common with them than you imagined. If so, I have written a hopeful book.

For your children

Chapter One:
Living the revolution now

When I stand directly in front of Eithin y Gaer homestead, it looks just like any other grey, Welsh, stone-built farmhouse. But if I walk round to the side and up the steep hill the difference looms imposingly. Behind the original house, and part of it, rises reputedly the biggest timber-framed house in Britain, and the home of a commune with the impressive name of Biotechnic Research and Development – BRAD for short.

In front of the house, beyond the farmyard and garden, rolling pasture and woodland fall away into the misty green valley far below, and beyond it great hills rise majestically out of the soft, spring mist. The occasional sounds – a dog barking in the distance, a lamb calling, a ringing axe – only emphasise the peace of the place. At the door of the house someone rings a handbell, and, one by one, a dozen or more people leave the work they are doing and gather for afternoon tea – today outside in the gentle sunshine. Eight adults and two children live here; the rest are, like myself, working visitors. The two children have scampered off, bread and jam in hand, to talk to Bambi the goat, and her two kids. Janine, Mike and Joanne amble up from the vegetable garden; Peter clambers down from the roof; John brings a huge brown teapot and dumps it on the tressle table, and Maria carefully places a freshly baked loaf of bread alongside it, for today has been their turn as commune cooks; Robin, who has been building a wall, washes some of the mortar off his hands. Except for Philip, away on a beekeeping course, the group is complete.

Teatime at Eithin y Gaer is a ritual break – often a time for an impromptu meeting to discuss some new project or raise a pressing problem. Today they discuss the three geese, Horace, Cynthia and Christmas Dinner. A few days ago rats ate six of Cynthia's goslings, and now with the remnants of her family she is temporarily in safer, but cramped housing. 'Horace isn't sleeping, he's worrying about Cynthia,' says Mike. 'We ought to get the new goose house fixed up so they can be reunited. It's not fair.' Discussion centres on how to build the new house from scrap and make it ratproof, a team of two members volunteers to start on it next day.

I learn that no one issues orders here, no formal plans are made or meetings called. A collective consciousness operates. No one is under any kind of external pressure. Each person knows what the commune is about. Everyone is aware of the dictates of the seasons, constraints of finance, lessons learned. Things happen roughly when they should, and the future evolves casually into the present.

Years ago Robin Clarke had a dream about a workable and preferable alternative to high industrial technology – long before the critical year, 1971, when the magazine he was editing, *Science Journal* met its demise and he found himself redundant. Once Robin and his wife, Janine, were freed of the need to conform, they worked steadily to transform the dream into a reality. There was much to do: they had to refine their aims, recruit like-minded people who would develop them further, find money and somewhere to do 'their thing'. Within a year they were well on the way, and they could envisage a community which would, as they wrote: '. . . seek to provide a new technology for people who wish to live in harmony with their environment, in peace with their neighbours, and in control of their lives and their technology.' The organisation would be dedicated to the search for techniques for fostering small-scale, rural community developments, using local resources and local labour. As they expressed it at the time: 'It hopes to be part of a process which will once again restore fertility, diversity and beauty to the land and provide satisfaction and happiness for its inhabitants by integrating them with their natural surroundings.'

As a disenchanted technocrat, Robin put technical things high on his list, and their first three priorities were to seek renewable energy sources, based on the sun, the wind and water power; find new ways to treat and use human, animal and plant wastes; and develop agricultural systems, growing many species of plants, fish, other animals and trees in an interdependent way with neither chemical sprays and fertilizers nor heavy, expensive equipment.

Plans crystallised: a nucleus of adventurers was formed and towards the end of 1972 they had pinpointed depopulated Montgomeryshire as their target. Robin and Janine journeyed there and within 3 days bought Eithin y Gaer for three good reasons: it was ecologically interesting with woodland, a stream and fantastic views; it was the right size – 44 acres; and it was the right price – £10,000.

By early 1973 an eight-bedroom, three-storey extension to the existing farmhouse had been architect-designed and approved by the planning authorities, and the first wave of communards was installed in tents and caravans. The house design included a solar roof to heat water; to heat the house itself, there was above-average insulation, and – working like a refrigerator in reverse – a heat pump to extract heat from a nearby stream and blow hot air throughout the house.

They had made their calculations with the same care as they had stated their aims and philosophies, but, on site, reality was different: chilly, muddy, chaotic and at times more than faintly ridiculous. As one member, Philip Brachi, put it: 'As yet we offer very little for the jobless of Workington, or the Dagenham man whose daily round consists of bolting fake air vents to the sides of the Ford Capri.'

Problems abounded. Planning permission had been won only because the new building was 'an extension to the existing dwelling'. It was some extension! Not only would it be four or five times the size of the little stone cottage, it would extend well into the hillside behind it. Time was of the essence, for the house must be habitable before winter; and so there was no alternative but to cheat: for £600 they hired a man and a bulldozer to excavate the site, and by spring 1973 the house began to take shape.

Summer saw work divided between the house and the vegetable garden, and by autumn the group gratefully forsook their tents and caravans and moved in. Apart from the bulldozer and one hired carpenter, all work had been voluntary and amateur, and the bill came to £10,000.

The house had been designed with eight double bedrooms and a capacity of sixteen people, but rather too neatly this anticipated eight couples, or fewer couples with children. Suitable recruits with suitable mates were not forthcoming, however, and the group that first wintered at Eithin y Gaer comprised eight adults and two children – Janine's and Robin's. Spare rooms were allocated to visitors.

Now in spring 1974 the dream is partially realised. Only one member of the original group has left, and two more have joined. The garden, which had supplied all their vegetables throughout the previous summer, has been enlarged and is now the centre of activity. The farm boasts 3 pregnant Jersey cows, 3 pigs, 7 assorted ewes and 9 lambs, Clarence the cock and his 23 hens, Bambi and her 2 kids, together with Horace, Cynthia, Christmas Dinner and the surviving goslings. Five acres of spring-sown barley, wheat and oats are already showing green.

Over tea I quiz Robin Clarke on technological progress, and I learn that for a variety of technical bureaucratic reasons, plans for re-using human waste had to be abandoned in favour of a conventional septic system, but the nitrogen-rich effluent is being led to the vegetable garden. Otherwise technical aspirations are part-fulfilled and unabated. A wind-powered pump pushes stream water uphill to a tank above house level. The 'windmill' is called a 'savonius rotor' – old 44-gallon oil drums cunningly cut and mounted on a vertical axis a dozen feet above the ground so that they scoop any available wind. 'It's a self-backing design,' Robin explains. 'The faster the wind blows the more back pressure is created and this prevents it from "undergoing catastrophic self-disassembly" – as the Americans put it.'

The solar roof is almost finished, I learn. In winter the roof of the house is shaded by the hill behind, but from late spring to early autumn it will heat large volumes of water to 'not very hot' and ease the load on a standard immersion heater. This roof will have cost around £350 for 65 square metres – a little more than any conventional non-solar roof.

The heat pump to heat the house from the stream will be installed during the summer. They hope to get an output of about 15 kilowatts from the input of 3 or 4 kilowatts needed to power the compressor – a gain of nearly five to one – and all for a total cost of about £350.

On the other side of the hill a completely autonomous house – solar heated and independent of outside power or water – will be built for a semi-separate community. They are looking for people to join it, and build the house with their own capital. 'It's very sophisticated and it'll cost a packet,' Robin adds.

The people melt away to continue with their various jobs until the bell rings again at 6 o'clock for supper. I give a hand building the new goose house.

Over the rest of the week the ambience of the community makes itself known to me as I share the workload, eat with its members, relax with them and talk with them one by one. I learn that soon after the group began functioning, the emphasis changed from solving technological problems to coping with psychological and sociological ones, also to becoming part of the local community. On this, Robin expressed his views emphatically when we talked later: 'The idea is not to build yourself a little castle, cut yourself off and grow everything from your pepper and salt down to your tobacco and pot. You really want to form a smaller type of society in which human interchange is very rich and grows – a "growth economy in human interchange" if you like. We find that happens here. Much of what we do here which is important is to do with the community outside our own community . . . integration with neighbours and the pub, the market, the school. In a sense I'd say that the thing that has worked best about our last year here has been the reception we've had – it's been incredible. I don't remember a single case of hostility.'

I learn something of the difficulties of living communally too – that visitors can be a problem, and that life in Eithin y Gaer has been likened to being in a railway station. I am impressed by the intense and strenuous 7-days-a-week activity, but I suspect that there may be too much of it; for although the pressures of straight society are noticeably absent, people admit to feeling guilty about taking time off. If a member wants to relax, in his room, or in one of the communal rooms, or on a hillside, even though he is perfectly entitled to do so, nevertheless it is difficult for him not to feel that he is shirking, and he senses that the rest of the group feel that he ought to be doing something. It seems too that ever-present activity, together with the constant flow of visitors, becomes an excuse for avoiding confrontation with human problems – whether those of the individual or relationships between members. The talk over meals and afterwards is bright and stimulating, but I am left wondering how much has been left unsaid.

I need reassuring too that they are more than affluent middle-class socialists using their money to buy their way out of the system rather than buy shares in this company or that. Is what I am witnessing a serious model of a new decentralist society – a cell which can multiply and offer a viable alternative to ecologically disastrous and consequently doomed cities? Or is it a fantasy trip – the new thing its members are 'into', an escape not only from the cities they have left behind, but a kind of group therapy to solve their personal problems and forget their inadequacies?

I stay the best part of a week there and, as we shall see later, I spend several hours with Robin and others talking about their aims, their plans and problems. It is an unforgettable week – a glimpse of another way to live – but it draws to a close and I find myself with them at supper for the last time. The bell has rung, a little after 6, and people are drifting in one by one to the huge baker's table at the back of the half-finished kitchen. The décor is drums of bulk food, rows of rubber boots, buckets, books, a notice-board, bags of cement, animal medicines, baby chicken behind a glass door, a deep-freeze, fluorescent strip lighting, bare walls and plumbing exposed, and a chiming clock. Sixteen people finally sit down, for there has been an influx of visitors. There is a preponderance of males, and among them a preponderance of beards. The three children are healthily boisterous. Although most people are hot, tired and hungry, the conversation crackles and vibrations are good humoured.

The two members who have been cooks for the day place big dishes of hot food around the table. Peter is still worried about a missing lamb, but Janine persuades him to have his supper before looking for it. 'It will probably turn up,' she reassures him, 'they usually do.'

Philip has returned, with 15,000 bees, and he describes how he hitch-hiked from London with them. 'Did you say what you were carrying?' someone asks him. 'Not exactly,' he replies, 'I said they were moles.' After supper he is going to transfer them from their carrying box to the hive. Anything could happen. Joanne is relieved he is back. While he was away, Bambi the goat swelled disconcertingly and the vet was called in. She was only slightly bloated, but Joanne was worried because Bambi is Philip's responsibility. There have been other problems too: the chicks have blood in their droppings. Each creature benefits from a copious outpouring of human concern.

Although the comments are rude to the point of coarseness, the food is excellent. Most meals are vegetarian, not from principle but necessity. Until their own animals are ready for killing, the protein input has to be eggs, cheese and beans. Expenditure is carefully watched. Running expenses for the whole community run at £250 a month, and that covers everything from food to fuel – everything except members' pocket money. Including an average of two visitors over and above the ten permanent members, this works out at just under £5 a person a week, of which

£2 is food. There is a 'food contribution' box for visitors prominently marked 'But only if you're rich'.

After supper Philip meticulously prepares for the drama of the bees. Everything is done calmly and quietly and in accordance with the course he has been attending. He emerges after taking a shower, dressed in his only clean clothes – white jeans and a pale blue cotton sweater. 'Bees have a keen sense of smell,' he explains. Hot water is poured into 6 pounds of precious sugar to make their syrup. 'They're hungry after the journey,' he tells us. He dons a hat and veil and climbs to the orchard, clutching a patent smoke generator and a screwdriver, and followed at a respectful distance by the spectators. There is a delay, for Maria has mistaken the steaming syrup for washing up water and poured soap powder in it. The calm in the interval is almost unbearable. Fresh syrup appears, the smoke generator is reluctantly coaxed into action and Philip unscrews the lid of the box in which the bees travelled. A dozen or so bees fly out sleepily and settle here and there. The remaining 14,988 cling to the removable sections of the box as he transfers each section in turn to the hive. In the middle of the operation someone forgetfully speaks. Philip straightens authoritatively: 'There must be no noise,' he says quietly. Gently he picks up the few remaining bees and one at a time pops them through a small hole in the hive, then places the lid on top. It is all over and the group relaxes. It is the first time he has done it, yet it is accomplished without orders, without fuss or reprimand, with excitement and with pleasure. They are everyone's bees – as it will be everyone's honey.

American Connection

To track down the survivalists I travelled from England, Scotland, and Wales across North America to the West Coast, seeking them in the countryside and cities. Some had left the cities either in hope or despair; others had elected to stay on and try to create places more fit for people than machines. I met some of those who stayed when I stopped over in Philadelphia at the end of the summer of 1973.

I find myself in the ample cellar-kitchen of a rambling old house in the shabby district of West Philadelphia. The cellar, like the rest of the house, is filled with second-hand furniture and home-made things, put together from scrap. It could not be called tidy, and yet it conveys a strong sense of order. Like the people I am to meet there, it is 'together'. George, Tony and I are sitting at the long, bare table, talking above the clatter of washing up. The evening meal was good and simple, enjoyed by a dozen people of all ages. Now some have gone upstairs to work or relax, a few talk good-humouredly as they do the dishes, and we three discuss the subject of revolution.

Before the meal I had been shown the neighbourhood, an in-between zone, bordered on one side by a predominantly black industrial district and on the other by a white one, sprinkled with university academics. The streets are wide and the houses are large and well proportioned, but peeling paint and broken windows help to tell the story of the place. Here and there a freshly painted house stands out, but the impression I get is of a place where people stay for a while and move on – a problem shared with much of urban Britain. In this neighbourhood a dozen or more houses serve as bases for a Quaker-inspired organisation known as the Life Centre. Each house is run as a separate commune, and the one called Stone House, where I am staying, is typical. I ask George Willoughby – a middle-aged, quiet but intense person – what the Life Centre is all about.

'Rather than just content ourselves with writing treatises about the coming revolution, we're trying, in a small way, to *live* the revolution now, and develop our own ideas to what is a better society,' he explains. 'We began here back in 1971, a group who'd been working together in peace and Civil Rights movements. We had gradually changed our viewpoints, believing that the world today – and American society especially – had got to the point where only radical change offered any hope. Several of us who felt this way left our work as teachers in universities – I had a Ph.D. and all that stuff – and one of our first steps was to set up the Life Centre, a community of support, work, learning and play.

'At the same time another group, the Movement for a New Society, was developing, spreading across the country and many other places in the world, and we linked with it. Its aim was to give a frame of reference for people who wanted to change the world and were willing to start changing themselves in the process. Basic to this is the idea that fundamental social change best comes through a non-violent approach, through people living and working together in community. There is no saviour for us – we've got to do it ourselves. We have to develop *now* the kind of economic and political system that we think is better.'

I interrupt: 'Fine words, but what are you yourselves in the Life Centre doing to bring this about?'

'We're changing our lifestyle,' he answers quickly, 'learning to live on less than we had before, sharing our goods so that we can live more economically; developing our own programmes of education and training for ourselves and for the community around us. We're quietly relating to the people in the neighbourhood around us as people who we're going to change, not by saying to them "Follow us, we have the way", but by example, by demonstration, by writing, by word of mouth, by ideas.

'We're experimenting with the whole idea of an egalitarian, highly decentralised society. Amongst other projects, we're beginning in a small way industries and businesses organised as collectives, because we think that people must be able to take control of their lives, to be responsible for themselves and each other.

'Above and around us the Great American Society is on the move, conditioned to accept the *status quo*. Down here a handful of idealists talk confidently about changing the world. They seem hopelessly outnumbered, committed to an impossible task, that is, unless I force myself to think of the connection between the acorn and the oak tree.'

I learn that the Life Centre is a purely Philadelphian phenomenon, and that although all its members belong to the Movement for a New Society (MNS), in other towns and cities the Movement takes different forms, with many but not all of its members living collectively. But in Philadelphia the Life Centre is the home of the MNS and more besides: it either runs or takes part in a wide range of community projects – a printing business, a food co-op, a home repair collective, a dental collective, a counselling service for people in distress, and a neighbours' association to fight local crime. Each of these diverse projects integrates the Life Centre with the neighbourhood, builds up a community spirit, and helps achieve the wider, long-term aims of the MNS (aims which we shall return to in Chapter Nine).

One of the projects, the Block Association of West Philadelphia – to give it its full name – was formed in January 1972 when, within 2 weeks, three women in the neighbourhood had been raped. The Association began as a means to fight crime, but became a way of giving back the streets to the people; helping them reject the barricade mentality of more locks, alarm systems, dogs and guns; helping them to lose their fear and draw closer together. Central to the scheme was a pocket-sized freon horn which lets out ear-piercing blasts when pressed. Each member of the community kept one handy as a means to alert others if in danger, or if anyone else were threatened. Volunteer teams of residents were formed to walk the streets in twos and threes, each 'armed' with the alarm-sounding horn. As George explains: 'People now realise that collectively they have power and can take responsibility for their block. Pushing that horn button is an action – it breaks the freeze of fear. They needn't be dependent on the police. Now they come out instead of cowering behind locked doors. People are helping each other again. This is a very important thing: that people should have a sense of the power to make decisions that affect themselves and their brothers and sisters. Working together with other people this power is more useful.'

I ask Tony Edgerton how he became involved and I learn that he had been working in the Government on the Poverty Programme until President Nixon froze the funds. So he quit and joined the Life Centre, working with the Neighbourhood Repair Collective. 'We're a group of up to twelve men and women that do our bread labour on all kinds of home repair,' he tells me. 'We share our skills among ourselves and also with the neighbourhood people we work for. We rotate and share our responsibilities, and decisions are made by the group, making sure everybody participates.' He explains how people in the neighbourhood gain a renewed sense of confidence when the Collective helps them develop the skills with their hands that enable them to repair their own homes. But the Collective aims for more than this, he stresses: 'Our long-term goal is to help people in the community come together around their problems and what's happening to housing in their immediate environment. And we help people get to know their legal rights about repairs in property they're renting.'

A young man joins us and George introduces him as Demi Miller, a member who worked for 2 years as a teacher in a school for blacks, and is now active in the food co-op. This was started to serve the Centre communes, but was always intended to grow and serve the neighbourhood too. Now there are eighty buying units registered with it, from the Centre's communes to families and single people, and they all benefit by getting better food at less cost. A collective of seven managers is paid a reasonable wage to run it and coordinate volunteers from the neighbourhood. 'As managers we set ourselves the goal to work ourselves out of a job,' he explains. 'If we get enough interested people we can encourage them to start their own co-ops, or divide ourselves in two: this idea of cellular division is better than just growing bigger and bigger.' I learn that the food co-op is a highly effective way of bringing together the people in the neighbourhood, and a chance to talk about the politics of the community, about American society, what's wrong with it and how the food co-op could be extended. George chimes in: 'Consciousness-raising, it's called: we used to call it "education".'

Demi is anxious to tell me about the counselling service for people in emotional distress. 'Re-evaluation Counselling', he calls it, and the way he describes it, succinctly, yet compassionately, makes sense – a means of helping people after a minimal amount of theoretical training. 'Co-counselling distributes resources the most effective way; it doesn't need a centralised person,' he explains. 'It is spread from person to person on a one-to-one basis. It has been going 20 years and we know it works.' He tells me how members try to reach distressed people in the community through all their contacts with it – from the house repair collective to the food co-op. 'You can detect the signals of distress that people give, even though we're all conditioned against admitting it,' he adds.

We talk about distress and from there to loneliness and the feeling experienced by so many people in cities that no one really cares, and again I see the parallel with problems in Britain and other countries. The chief difference seems to be that – as in so much of America – everything is bigger. On one point we agree: that society is sick, even though we see it in different terms. I ask George for his view.

'I think much of its sickness lies in its sheer *bigness*,' he replies. 'Its massive wealth, its corruption and concentration of power – all in the name of the virtue of a democratic, free society built upon individualism. Now this has a lot of value in it, but it has gone to the extreme point where many of us have literally imprisoned ourselves out in the suburbs in our little houses and retreated there. They've become the cells we've built for ourselves so that we can run away from the world – a society that is utterly inhuman in many ways, and one we have no control over. Some people are finding that even in the confines of their own homes there is no freedom – that we can't get along without other people. And so a few are beginning to come out again.'

I stay over in the Stone House collective and spend a day while they join other collectives to talk through problems of administration and objectives. The day is characterised by gaiety and earnestness, frankness, open criticism and occasional – apparently sincere – praise. Decisions are made by consensus – nobody is ignored and the method *works*. But these people bear no resemblance to the majority around them. They are white, middle-class, educated and dedicated. Can they really bridge the yawning gulf to reach the black, poor and ignorant? And what of the other impediments – the rival propaganda from the imposed society which promises Utopia through 'the mixture as before'? Will the Life Centre and the Movement for a New Society be no more effective than the disregarded health hazard warning on a packet of cigarettes – puny against the weight of tobacco publicity and intensive lobbying?

The Loners

Not every survivalist lives in a commune – far from it. Communal living makes sense: in constant, close contact with others, self-deception becomes harder to maintain, and loneliness ceases to be a major problem. It is a cheaper way to live too, and by 'locking you into the system' less, it is a liberating influence. Moreover it is a far less wasteful way of living for it saves fuel, space and materials, and so is kinder to the environment. As the crisis deepens, communal living may prove to be the key to mankind's survival but it demands heavy sacrifices which not everyone is able to make: loss of privacy and possessions, unselfishness and total commitment – to name a few. When it works it is a beautiful experience, but it is not necessarily the right way for those who have been too long in the imposed society.

Two people who tried it and turned away from it are Dammy and John Manson. Now, with their two small children they farm a remote 6-acre croft in Aberdeenshire. To see John sweating as he scythes pasture for the hay that will feed his goats, you would hardly connect him with the backroom scientist, a neurophysiologist, who spent years researching, studying the workings of the brain. Nor would you connect Dammy, baking in an antique stove in the hot, cluttered kitchen, with the Kensington-born, trainee-buyer at Harrods, who once immersed herself in Women's Lib. But here they both are, at the end of a period of change which began 6 years ago, and living in a way which rejects just about everything they had been conditioned to accept. I ask John how things are panning out, and he stops his work to answer me. 'We've been here nearly 3 months,' he says. 'It's back-breaking and exhausting – surely neolithic man was better organised for farming than we are at present. But we have things in the ground, gardens dug, oats planted, silage and some hay made already; and the goats arrive this week. It's good – as good as it ought to be and perhaps better: better as we get more confidence in ourselves and learn or remember, or read more, or listen to neighbours – who are slightly unbelieving but none the less friendly. We're penniless but happy. We've no complaints.'

The air coming in from the sea is cool and sweet even though the sun burns hot in the bright, clear light. Beyond their gently sloping pasture runs a small stream. Woodland surrounds the croft. I suspect that the hills and the sense of distance remind John of his native New Zealand. This year the spring and early summer have been dry, meaning work in the fields from early morning until 10 or later to make the most of long northern evenings. But when the rain finally comes, squally and soaking, it drives them reluctantly into the long, low farmhouse: John and Dammy then have time to tell me something of their old life and the changes which led them here.

John speaks first, frowning as he forces his mind back to a time he would rather forget. 'You don't exactly choose your work in the sense that you *decide* to be a lecturer in a medical school,' he says, picking his words carefully. 'Provided the nose is kept well clean, there's a natural progression from undergraduate, through postgraduate research, postdoctoral fellowships and so on, and then – with the appropriate grooming for the horse-trading market – you get a lectureship. By then you've a well-developed, well-nurtured ambition, and you quickly suppress any passing doubts as you gnaw at the next carrot – be it more research, finance, bigger and better equipment or a higher academic appointment. I'm not sure where my programming went wrong . . . early potty training not quite rigorous enough I suppose. I went into research with fairly high ideals, and I think I really did hope to be some use to people when their heads went wrong. But it's pretty difficult to keep the ideals topped up at full strength when they're contaminated by nasty reality: the necessary ambition, the drive to publish – almost anything will do – the round of conference appearances, and to join – and be seen to have joined – the right learned societies.' He recalls his time in a research institute, his repugnance of constant vivisection and a nagging worry about the use or misuse to which his discoveries might be put – in short his growing disillusionment. 'I shall always remember a nurse who short-circuited all the polite conventions people use when they want to know how a scientist spends his time; she simply asked "What have you found out?" Now what kind of ridiculous question is that? One doesn't *find out*, one is working on, or researching into, or looking at the possibility that, and so on and so on . . . I seriously began to question what I was doing, why and who for, and whether it wasn't really some kind of intellectual masturbation. And all condoned by a society which hadn't yet woken up to its priorities – or more probably one which was deliberately kept in ignorance against the day when it might question the use to which vast sums of money were being put by its Glorious Scientists – or by this one, anyway!'

He recalls how he searched for a political position which made sense, but found little among the various sects. 'The threads of decentralist politics were milling round in my mind; something like the Libertarian Eco-anarchist cum Agrarian Reform Party might have filled the bill, but I didn't know the words at the time. It was a depressing period. Most of the societal models I'd accepted seemed pretty tatty. I reckoned that either I was surrounded by decaying institutions, mainly dedicated to maintaining a *status quo* which I found increasingly repellent, or else my view of the world had become twisted and I needed a course of the little red and green ones. It was Dammy and a few close friends who persuaded me that my doubts weren't necessarily the signal for "chemo-therapeutic socialisation". You must remember that most of this happened about 6 years ago, before it was fashionable to have doctrinal doubts, and there weren't many people to talk about it. Without Dammy's support I'm not sure

I'd have coped. As one friend put it, I didn't fit any more. And I didn't want to either. Finally a rather nasty little bit of academic politics put the seal on it . . . it's a bitchy world, academics; so is the theatre, but the girls are prettier. I decided to get out.'

The Mansons began a search for what John calls 'a believable alternative', first within conventional career structures and then to less conventional alternatives. As part of his embryonic plan he began to learn leathercraft in his spare time. All the while he was aware that a whole bunch of ideas was coming together: politics, the environment, energy resources, personal liberation and other decentralist themes. 'They fell into place,' he explains, 'after I'd read the first newsletter from the New Alchemists in America; it was called "A Modest Proposal". I wrote to them and to BRAD, and I gradually infiltrated the alternative technology network. I went to work for a week at BRAD, planted a lot of potatoes and got my head straight. When I came back Dammy and I decided to try and get a group together, or join an already existing one. We wanted to see if we could get this whole idea of self-sufficiency in food and energy off the ground.'

The idea of a community seemed imperative, even though neither of them felt they were born communards. They tried to form first one group and then another, but both attempts foundered, chiefly on the question of the degree of communality. John explains: 'We felt you have to give every chance for a group "thing" to develop – I can't define it, but it's powerful and worth working for once you experienced it. But the others wanted to eat and cook separately which seemed to us to be ecologically and economically wasteful, as well as, quite simply, "un-fun".'

Despite this setback, they pressed on; John resigned his job, they sold their Edinburgh flat and they moved in on some obliging friends. As John put it: 'We weren't in the mood for another love affair. It seemed more important to get our hands dirty, not just talk about organic farming, solar heaters and the like, but to go and bloody do it! After a 2-month search we found this 6-acre croft – which we couldn't afford – and bought it.'

'You've got guts,' I interject, 'you've not picked a cushy life;

but, all the same, isn't what you're doing an élitist thing – something you chiefly want to do for your own sakes without any wide implications?'

'We're lucky,' John admits. 'Let's not mince words, 10 years in the system, capital from selling the flat, cashing insurance policies and a small legacy enabled us to buy our way out! But I don't think we have to dash to the nearest supplier of hair shirts to expiate a middle-class guilt. What it does add up to is a responsibility to turn outwards in every way we can, rather than inwards on ourselves and watch the oats grow. We're still looking for the most practical way of doing this . . . possibly developing into a larger group and widening our base and so our usefulness generally. Or perhaps by being a place where people can come and pick up skills before doing it themselves somewhere – or both. At present we're still trying to sum up the potential of the land and buildings.'

They realise that they will need a small income and they hope that it will come from the leathercraft work. This could be a problem, as John recognises: 'So far I've only sold my stuff through the protected environment of my tutor's shop. I've yet to find markets here, which may well be the difficult part. The other problem is finding time to do the work. When we finish outside around 10 or 11 in the evening as we often do, it requires something superhuman in the way of energy to sit down and start making leather goods!'

'Surely there's a danger,' I suggest, 'that you'll always be too spent or short of time to do any serious alternative technology – you'll just remain subsistence crofters.'

He ponders the thought carefully: 'We clearly recognise that we're at the "simple" end of the alternative technology scale, and for myself, instead of devising a wind-powered, solar-heated Savonius grasscutter, I'm happiest grabbing a scythe and getting on with it. Revisionist pig! I suspect that, for some people, there could be a danger of regarding alternative technology as an end in itself, whereas it is but the technology of decentralisation. In the life I foresee for ourselves there'll be a mixture of relearning old skills, borrowing from other cultures and perhaps inventing a new technique or two in passing. And yes, windmills and solar heaters breaking the horizon. It doesn't easily lend itself to definition, nor perhaps should it. Maybe we *are* simply crofters.'

Dammy has been with us for some of the time in between looking after the kids and the kitchen. Now she has settled down to join us. 'I'm not sure whether I'm a "detail" of John's or not,' she begins lightly; and as she continues I learn that she had been highly 'career motivated' until she met John, but London social life was already beginning to pall. 'John was busy going somewhere,' she explains, 'so I went with him, and on the way I learned how to think, while he was also learning. Two years living in Oxford showed me how grey the Great White God of science really was, but I was still sure John's part in it was worthwhile. By the time our son was expected, John was well on the way to some change of direction, but I was lagging behind. I knew that all the things he was saying were true, but I didn't feel a great need to change my own life – I was too absorbed with the kids, and he was pretty lonely for a long time. Eventually I got some energy back and I began to go to Women's Lib meetings. Talking at them began to give me back some confidence in myself and I started to experience the "highs" of self-discovery. At the same time, John was becoming clearer about what he wanted to do and we started to work out our future plans together. The idea of community fitted in very well with my feelings of liberation.

'By now I was beginning to feel that "the women's problem" was only part of the sickness of industrialised society. Although the fight for women's human rights and dignity still seemed worthwhile, I was more and more seeing a basic philosophy of life differently from fellow "women's libbers". To encourage women to fight for the equal opportunity to work seemed to me to be adding to the problem rather than dealing with it in any way. I felt that there was a more valuable "subversive" role to play, shaping one's children's attitudes before they're claimed by the educational system for 8 hours a day.'

Earlier in the day, Dammy had told me how she had helped

John rake about a ton of stones from a field before they could sow their acre of corn, and how she had helped him roll it afterwards – hauling an old milk churn filled with the stones. I wondered how much of her idealism had stayed with her now she had elected to become a 'crofter's wife'. When I asked her she replied without hesitation. 'Now after 3 months of what you could call very "unliberated" work, I feel less conflict about my own roles than I've felt for years. There's still the tug between inside and outside work – which one takes priority? – but that's also getting less. Although my life is much more like that of a Victorian farmer's wife, I feel an increased sense of my own importance in the scheme of things. You soon learn that it's pointless to wish you had the strength to scythe all day: I don't have that strength and it's far more efficient for one person to take charge of food preparation anyway. Priorities soon work themselves out: hay has to be got in before the weather breaks, so the house gets chaotic, but as long as we still eat enough, who cares? I appreciate John's work and effort, and he appreciates mine, so "liberation" no longer seems a meaningful phrase.'

'The way you talk,' I say, 'makes it seem as if the change from your old life to this one has been all too easy . . .'

Dammy pulls me up short: 'It was extremely difficult to start changing from city attitudes towards something else; but that hackneyed old phrase about living on the land seems to take on a new meaning when you're actually *doing* it. The changing seasons, your dependence on the weather and the soil to grow food soon put you in your place – and fairly low in the scale of things. But it's a lot less frustrating to have an escaped cow trample on the seed beds than to have a quarrel with petty officialdom in some post office. The pigeons may take a whole row of newly-planted seedlings, but you can make more headway fighting off pigeons than getting angry with faceless government decisions – and make more immediate point.'

I sense that the time allowable for talking is drawing to a close: rain may be holding up farm activities, but indoors a backlog of weeks has piled up. 'What about the criticism of élitism?' I ask.

'We can't hope to grow food for the starving millions,' Dammy answers, 'but we *can* hope to relearn the knowledge of our grandparents, and about how to live in harmony with our natural environment instead of raping it with monocultures, herbicides, artificial fertilisers and all the other products of a marketing man's paradise. We hope to find that *some* of our education can be put to good use, and if we can combine it with laterally thinking minds, we can evolve a way of living which we can usefully communicate to other people. At least what we learn won't be locked away in some dusty library about how people "used to live"; and if we can pass some of our newly acquired wisdom to our children, they'll be better equipped to survive the next century. We'll never achieve all that we've set out to achieve, but at least we'll feel that we're going in the right direction.'

The Growing Minority
Robin Clarke in Wales and George Willoughby in Philadelphia, with their fellow communards, and Dammy and John Manson in Scotland on their own, are not just isolated crackpots. Word is getting around that there are increasingly respectable alternatives to the 'straight', nine-to-five society; and in a host of different ways, people are questioning, protesting, dropping out or getting involved.

Not long ago this irreverent behaviour was strictly for youth, a sprinkling of academics and a few other thinkers or poets; the establishment found this disquieting, but no great threat, for its members were lulled by the lessons of history. It seems that, although every age had its dissenters, the establishment has generally managed not only to withstand incessant pinpricks, but even to ward off the odd savage thrust.

Sometimes, however, when the society under attack is crumbling or corrupt, irreverent questioning proves to be the first sign of serious cracks in its foundations – cracks with a tendency to spread rapidly unless smartly sealed, and accompanied by an all-out effort to buttress the society's main structure. A good deal of evidence is around that 'Western' society is at just such a moment in history, and a close look at some of the questioning reveals much.

So long as most of the dissent came from youth, today's increasingly industrial society has barely flinched. Protest has been seen as a healthy stage in growing up: an interlude for youth to smoke and talk without ever getting anywhere no matter how much they bummed around. A few months or years of opting out posed no lasting threat so long as youth had no lasting alternative to opt into. Predictably, each wave of young dissenters eventually found places on the industrial treadmill, however reluctantly, with little worse to show for the experience than long hair and a penchant for the occasional joint.

But more recently something more significant has been happening. Dissenting youth has begun to acquire odd bedfellows: older people have been sensing that the imposed, industrial society – to which they had been connected without specifically dialling it – was somehow failing to deliver the promised fun. 'Life is great in the great consumer society' the politicians and publicists went on asserting, yet reality was failing to correspond: the present was revealing itself as tawdry and unjust, while the future was beginning to look ever more bleak.

People, old enough to know better, began acting strangely. Some escaped to small farms and the elusive ideal of self-sufficiency; some inserted quaint advertisements in respectable papers, seeking others to join them in rural communities; some stayed in the towns and cities and gave up all or part of their time from producing ever-more goods and services and began helping those who found themselves unable to cope with this 'imposed society'; some joined revolutionary movements – mostly non-violent; the technically-minded in town and country began experimenting in alternative technologies to produce energy from the sun, the wind, rivers and tides – even from sewage and manure; some started underground papers on miniature presses, taking over where the once-fiery student papers had left off; some set off to fight world poverty; some instead stayed at home, devoting their spare time and energy to focus attention on pollution and the squandering of world resources; some did all this and more.

Yet they were still a small minority. Most folk went about their work as before. An optimist among the minority might cherish a hope that in some way the majority were subtly changed – dimly aware perhaps that, beneath the veneer of the imposed society, cracks were growing which one day they might have to heed. The optimist might believe that one day his fellow freaks would be found to be right: that the cracks were growing too fast to plaster over, that the whole massive edifice might collapse.

Although this eccentric minority is unorganised, although its members rarely meet each other and have no agreed manifesto, they seem to share a belief that society needs to do a U-turn. They all hold that the world is in much more of a mess than most people realise, and is almost certainly hell-bent on oblivion. Many of them believe this disaster course is chiefly due to the industrial activities of a few extremely rich nations, busily exploiting the poor nations. They perceive the driving force behind this activity as technology, misapplied in the pursuit of greed.

They share the view that the necessary U-turn cannot be made without political change. Mostly they believe that capitalism as it has evolved is on the way out – and in need of more than a gentle nudge towards the exit. It is axiomatic that any body, which places the prosperity of its shareholders above the needs of its workers *as people*, of mankind in general, or the biosphere, is an anachronism. Politically most survivalists are well left of centre, but they find no solace in old-time Marxism; neither do any of the conventional political parties enjoy their support – not one of them admits to the impossibility of everlasting economic growth, nor has come out with an alternative policy to safeguard the least privileged from inevitable repercussions. Their economic policies, as one survivalist has observed, are obsessed with rearranging the deck chairs on the Titanic.

To a man – and woman – they see mankind as sick, a species whose dominant members are preoccupied with changing the planet and shortening its life span, mostly for short-term profit. A few members of the species – a minority as yet weak and divided – are opposing this process. The cure, they say, lies not in straining after more and more of everything in a fruitless attempt to satisfy an insatiable appetite, but to use accumulated knowledge differently; to share, rather than compete; to live in harmony with nature rather than exploit it. Needless to say, to the upholders of conventional wisdom, it is a point of view which sounds like standing reality on its head.

Because this eccentric minority is chiefly concerned with survival – either their own or that of others – I have called its members 'The Survivalists'. As I have said, over the past year I travelled many thousands of miles to meet a cross-section of them, and this book tells of their work and why they do it. They are part of the maligned and suspect 'alternative society'. Life in the alternative can be warmer or colder than in the imposed society, but it is seldom more comfortable. It is however always *different*, and most of the people I met there were free of the tensions and frustrations of imposed society, though it would be untrue to describe them as happy. Sadly, instead, many of them were disheartened, for Utopia remained persistently at the end of the rainbow. Too often precious energy was dissipated in squabbling and bungling; significant lessons from history were ignored; readily available 'establishment expertise' was spurned, no matter how relevant; squalor was prevalent – even revered; educated middle-class whites predominated, with inevitable pockets of élitism; miracles were prematurely claimed; like God, the much abused 'system' was readily sought in times of trouble . . . Problems abounded: they were simply different ones. Yet no one I met wanted to go back. In a way there is no turning back, for as one survivalist put it: 'You suddenly realise – there is no alternative but the alternative.'

These people may be significant prophets, or they may simply be working out their own psychological problems, and in the book I shall try to distinguish one from the other.

Survival means different things to different people: to some it is the possibility of shivering, miserably cold and under-fed, through yet one more day; to others it is realising one's potential as a fulfilled, creative human being; some are concerned only with their own skins, others have wider horizons: their family, community, country . . . all mankind . . . *all* life. To some the issue is one of feeding all those alive today; while others reflect wistfully on the consequences for future generations if we were to do so.

If the book has an aim, it is to shift the focus of attention from a preoccupation with trivia to a confrontation with reality. It hopes to do so in a way that reflects the excitement, happiness and disappointment felt by this eccentric minority which believes it might be learning to tell the difference between the two.

Chapter Two:
The sickness and the cure

Like other creatures, we all have basic needs which must be satisfied if we are to survive. One of the chief differences between us and them is the number of these needs and their complexity: we would have about as much difficulty accommodating to the simple life-style of an amoeba as the amoeba would if it tried to build a house.

Without getting lured down the thorny path of Arguments about Evolution, it is fairly safe to state that we are social animals: most of us prefer to live and work with others and so we tend to create societies. These societies must satisfy our basic needs: if they fail to do so, something has to give – either the society undergoes change, or its members find their survival threatened.

Without getting lured too far down the other thorny path of psychology, let us take a commonsense look at some of our basic needs, so that presently we may see how well or badly today's imposed society satisfies them for most of its members.

For health we need basically fresh air, food, water, sleep, shelter and warmth. So far so good: but the health of a complex organism such as man insists that less tangible needs are also satisfied; and dangerous though it may be to list them, not least because they overlap, we must have a try.

We need security. We yearn to love and be loved – not forgetting love of ourselves if we are to be capable of loving others. We are unlikely to feel secure unless we sense that we belong somewhere – in a place, or as a member of a group, or enjoying the knowledge that we have earned some kind of status.

We need some control over our lives and surroundings, so that we are not tossed constantly this way or that by other people and events. Security is important to us for so many reasons, not least because it helps us to build an identity, the feeling of being a real person with the assured knowledge that we really do exist. But too much security can threaten survival. And so in a real world we are constantly confronted by threats which demand a swift response. Consequently we have an inbuilt need to meet challenges with action, to be creative, to reproduce and enjoy doing so.

Most of us feel a need to work, although we may be turned off the idea when it conflicts with our needs for creativity and stimulation: for example when it is fruitless or boring. While at work, and in other situations, we have a strong need to be able to *cope* – to experience physical or mental challenge and to meet it effectively; neither winning nor losing every time, but discovering in the activity a sense of identity and the feeling of being in control.

We all need stimulation, some more than others. Stimulation runs parallel with challenge and certainly involves sex. It implies the presence of change – a change of place, of habits, of ideas; but always in the right dose. Too much or too rapid change and we lose our essential sense of security and ability to cope.

Some of us need a sense of aesthetics. Possibly as children we all knew this, but for many of us it withers with time, crowded out by other more urgent, easily satisfied needs. But it is strong when it is present, and when those who have held on to it are deprived of it, they are prone to other deprivations too – of identity, security, creativity and sensitivity.

The list is debatable, and demonstrably incomplete, but it is a guide which will do for our immediate purpose; to establish what we need for survival and to assess how well the society, which has been imposed on us, manages to satisfy them.

But before then, let us take a look at the needs of the planet which sustains us and our society.

We have needs: the planet also has needs. If they are in harmony, well and good, but if they are in conflict, once again something has to give: at best, either we must learn to live with modified needs, or in a modified planet; at worst, as a species we will disappear, leaving as our monument an empty planet.

The Mantle of Life

Around the Earth is a thin envelope in which life exists. It rises to some 25,000 feet in the air and 30,000 feet down into the oceans, while under dry land it is only a few feet deep. Although measurements in thousands of feet may suggest an impressively deep layer, in relation to the size of the planet, this envelope is no more than a thin, delicate film. The part of it which supports life was identified a century ago and given the name 'the biosphere'. It is 2 or 3 billion years old and it could continue indefinitely. But to do so, its basic needs must be satisfied. And just as man's needs are complex in comparison with those of the amoeba, those of the biosphere are as complex as one would expect for a system so dazzlingly and spectacularly diverse. To describe this miracle, so fragile, and possibly unique, as a 'system' is to sound prosaic, yet system it is. The energy on which it depends comes almost entirely from the sun; it is distributed by the atmosphere and the oceans and then re-radiated into space as heat. Only a fraction of 1 per cent of this energy remains to sustain life, 'fixed' principally by green plants and algae, by the miraculous process of photosynthesis, which literally brings dead matter to life. These plants and algae grow, die and decay and so provide food for other species such as man, animals and bacteria – creatures which can only live off the sun's energy second-hand. When they die, their bodies re-enter the system along with dead plant matter, forming part of an infinite number of food chains, all cyclic and all of them connected to each other. Normally nothing in the system is ever wasted, and nothing is ever created which survives to endanger the food chains.

All life has basically the same needs: energy from the sun

(either direct or second-hand), oxygen, water, and not too much variation in temperature.

The system is constantly changing, yet it has a double insurance against major harm: the enormous diversity of species and their capacity to adapt to change. Moreover change, however profound, is not normally rapid: the protective mantle of cloud, water vapour and gases of the atmosphere – themselves dependent on the photosynthesis of plants – keep the temperature of the biosphere constant enough for life to thrive. And thrive it could, for just as long as the energy from the sun continues to reach it.

As George M. Woodwell, Senior Ecologist at Brookhaven National Laboratory in the USA, has described the process: 'If one were to ascribe a single objective to evolution, it would be the perpetuation of life. The entire strategy of evolution is focused on that single end . . . the entire process appears to be open-ended, continuous, self-augmenting and endlessly versatile. It builds on itself, not merely preserving life, but increasing the capacity of a site to support life.'

Some of the biosphere's basic needs now become clear: the sun's energy; the protective filter of the upper atmosphere; the mantle of gases, water vapour and cloud beneath; oxygen and water available for all life forms; photosynthesis by green plants and algae; controlled temperature; uninterrupted food chains; the fully cyclic process of birth, death, decay and rebirth; conservation of finite resources; absence of rapid or widespread change with unpredictable repercussions; diversity of species to cushion change; ability of species to adapt to change; conditions for the interdependence of different species to flourish. Allow the biosphere these needs, and life may continue indefinitely: deny them and it ends.

Our tentative list of man's needs seems reasonable enough: given his ability to limit his numbers they present no obvious threat to the biosphere's survival. And yet an uncomfortable feeling is growing that something has gone terrifyingly wrong. G. Evelyn Hutchinson, Sterling Professor of Zoology at Yale University, voiced this when he said in 1970: 'Many people . . . are concluding on the basis of mounting and reasonably objective evidence that the length of life of the biosphere as an inhabitable region for organisms is to be measured in decades rather than hundreds of millions of years. This is entirely the fault of our own species.'

Need versus Greed

The biosphere, it seems, can take care of our needs, but not the onslaught of our wants – or, less kindly, our greed. Greed may be an ancient vice, but it now has powerful allies in science and technology. And, as the survivalists seem to put it, no force has so much shaped our society as these allies, misapplied in the pursuit of greed. It may not be the *only* ruinous force around, but it is the one which spawned the consumer society based on limitless economic growth, and the myth that happiness is to be found in the endless pursuit of stimulation and materialism. And all within a finite world that must somehow yield unlimited goodies forever.

As a species we differ from the others with whom we share the biosphere – those which seem to have posed no threat to its existence during the past 2 or 3 billion years. The difference lies not only in the *complexity* of our needs, but in at least one other significant way. When a tiger has fed, it dozes, and its prey are safe until it is hungry again; a bird which has built its nest has no desire for a 'second home'; the soft hermit crab stays in its acquired, protective shell until it has outgrown it and finds another; no creature intentionally kills its own kind once submission signals have been conveyed. We are different because we do not know when to stop. It is as if some insatiable curiosity compels us relentlessly to extend our senses until we lose the distinction between needs and wants. If this distinction is important for the biosphere's future, it could be helpful to try listing our wants in the same way that we have tried to summarise our needs.

Most wants within the imposed society can be identified as needs, exploited for profit. In our money-oriented economy our inability to know when to stop becomes the mainspring which powers the philosophy of unlimited growth, and any one of our needs, whether physical or spiritual, is fair game for exploitation. Consider the basics of food, water, sleep, shelter, and warmth. Over-eating has become a major killer, palate titillation is a major industry, along with advertising and packaging – the cost of which often exceeds the value of the food itself. Water is now a rare drink, for all industrial countries are completely hooked on beverages, mostly stimulants marketed with 'psychological extras'. Sleep has generated a diffuse market, from posture mattresses, water-beds and duvets to the lucrative and ever-growing sleeping pill business. Meanwhile shelter and warmth have become the biggest status symbol market of all – industries oblivious to the infiniteness of the essential resources on which they depend: land, materials, and energy.

When we consider the less tangible, or spiritual, needs, the same pattern of perversion and exploitation is evident. Deprived of community we surround ourselves with possessions to reinforce our shaky sense of identity and buttress our flagging feelings of security. Our competitive, achievement-oriented society exploits the work ethic, glorifying work for its own sake, and fighting against the effect of automation by creating employment, whether its end-products are useful or not. Upon the need for stimulation largely depends the giant industries of entertainment and escapism, from pop music to packaged tours. And sex, which had once been a private affair between two people, has not only exploded into an industry in its own right, but pervaded the marketing of almost every product you care to name.

The catalogue of wants appears as a motley collection, yet a common thread runs through it. Significantly most of them involve making products and exploiting people and nature – or both.

There is a simple test any of us can do if we want to begin distinguishing between needs and wants. Walk through your home with a pad and pencil, and make an inventory of the things you could do without and still be as happy as you are. Or if you prefer, list the things you would need to keep, remembering to include the car in your judgement. When this is done, contemplate the materials and fossil fuel which have been expended in making, delivering and running the things you don't really need. Then imagine several million others throughout the affluent, industrial nations, all doing the same test, and consider how much of the planet would have been left intact if these things had never been made; or, if you prefer, dwell on the suffering that might have been alleviated if the same materials and energy had been spent on meeting the needs of a billion or more of the world's most desperately poor. Finally cast your eye over the things you feel you must keep if you are to be happy, and contrast it with the possessions of the unfortunate billion.

A group of frugal young people living communally in Berkeley, California, in a house called Village Design, where I lived for a while, graphically describes this sobering experience. From your home 'take out all furniture,' they say, 'except a few old blankets, a mat, one table and a chair; take away all clothing except your oldest dress, a suit, and one pair of shoes for the head of the family; remove the pantry and the kitchen, leave a small bag of flour, some sugar, salt, a few potatoes, and a handful of dried beans for the night's supper; dismantle the bathroom, remove all the electricity; cancel all newspaper, magazine, and book club subscriptions; your family is illiterate. There is one radio for the entire town. Remove the postman, fireman, any public service. Move the school at least 5 miles away; cut it down to two rooms, enough for less than half the children, move the nearest clinic 10 miles away. Replace the doctor with a midwife; throw away bank books, stock certificates, pension plans, insurance policies. Leave the family a cash hoard of 5 dollars; move the family to a tool shed. Take away the house. Replace 10,000 neighbouring houses with shanties. Cut off 25 to 30 years of life expectancy.'

If you have been in the homes of people so poor – as I have done – you expect to find them far more miserable than they are. Yet laughter, love, trust and spontaneity abound. To point out that they escape many of the problems of affluence – obesity, psychosomatic illness, depression, misanthropism, anxiety, loneliness, restlessness, violence, to name a few – is not to offer any defence of the obscenity of modernised poverty. What it helps to emphasise is just how few wants are truly necessary for the elusive condition called happiness. When it comes to the crunch, not many wants are either culturally or intellectually stimulating, and all are 'open ended' – that is to say there is no assurance that satisfying a want will put an end to desire, either for more of the same, or for something different. More often the opposite happens! In one recent piece of research among Americans with a wide span of incomes, *all* reckoned that a satisfactory income was 25 per cent more than they were getting already!

And this is the rub. This is where the biosphere begins to wince, as a couple of examples will show.

In Britain and the USA up to one-fifth of all national output is in one way or another involved in moving goods and people from one place to another. This questionable activity – the consequence of increasing centralisation – involves mining vast quantities of finite resources and using limited reserves of fuel, not only to make aircraft, ships and vehicles but also to run them; it pollutes the air, land and oceans with dangerous poisons; it covers scarce land with millions of acres of concrete, and – as if that were not enough – jeopardises the protective upper atmosphere into the bargain.

Before the end of the century, on present trends, most of the world's population will live in cities. Cities grow because of the opportunities they present for gaining power, money and status symbols – for competition and a host of other kinds of stimulation. They suck in from the countryside millions of people in search of work as their local industries and communities wither and die, and as people leave the land, their place is taken by products: machines and chemicals. Farming becomes 'agribusiness', the land a factory floor, and the repository of a frightening array of chemical fertilisers, poisons and heavy machinery, exported from the cities without regard for the sensitive food chains of living processes of the soil beneath. To resist the ensuing build-up of pests and diseases, plant breeders concentrate on producing new strains of crops; diversity is lost, and the production of food, on which the overgrown cities so critically depend, becomes increasingly vulnerable.

The survivalists condemn the monoculture of a money-oriented economy in which growth becomes the overriding aim: in such an economy cities, governments, companies and industries must all keep growing, in the manner of the cells of cancer, to satisfy ever-escalating, but never fulfilled, wants and to swell the hypnotic Gross National Product.

The survivalists maintain that in the pursuit of industry we have set ourselves at loggerheads with nature, declaring that, if we fail to meet the needs of the biosphere, the biosphere cannot respond to meet *our* needs. If we divert human and other resources from satisfying needs to chasing wants, they say, we must expect to pay the consequences. Perhaps there would be some remote justification in reducing the biosphere to rubble if it were all in a worthy cause: say the creation of a Utopia where, at least for a few hundred years, our species could flower, beautifully and happily, before vanishing. Utopia however is a place where our needs are satisfied, and there is no evidence that the road we have chosen will lead us any closer to finding it.

Within our imposed society we concentrate on stimulating wants – which can never be satisfied – to the neglect of satisfying needs. Denied this basic satisfaction, we try to forget the loss – by chasing after more and more wants.

Defenders of this society pin their faith in technology and growth to reduce its imperfections, calling for patience, work, and ever more technology as the way to climb out of the difficulty. This, however, leaves the survivalists singularly unconvinced. They say that technology has got into the hands of people who have their priorities all wrong. Ever more technology – even in the right hands – they claim is too naïve a solution, and they come back to the idea that society has to do a quick U-turn. Inevitably they question the profit motive which powers the whole Western-style industrial system. They say that with such a motivation it is unsurprising that at best only *some* needs for *some* of the people are ever satisfied; and when they *are* satisfied it is only incidentally, as a sort of by-product of the profit system.

One such survivalist is Peter Harper, a young scientist who did 4 years graduate research in the application of biochemical methods to learning and behaviour, and then, disenchanted with formal research, 4 years ago devoted his full energies to the search for new solutions to the problems faced by a society coping with scientific-technical progress. He highlights the danger in allowing technology free growth, pointing out how it starts 'a compelling dialectical dance with the social and political institutions', making demands which in effect take over the whole values and mood of society. When this happens, the sensitive critic 'sees his every dream being thwarted or perverted. He wants socialism, he gets technocracy, he wants equality, he gets hierarchies; he wants control, he gets bureaucracies, he wants comprehension, he gets jargon; he wants community, he gets dormitory suburbs; he wants joy in work, he gets unemployment or commuting; he wants clean air, he gets a smog-mask.'

Conditioned to Accept
Of all the human needs which today's mass society fails to meet, two stand out from the rest: love and a sense of belonging. Almost every day the ordinary citizen meets more people than he can possibly get to know; and, with time at a premium, we treat each other, more as economic functions, less as fragile, fellow humans. If coping with so many people is onerous, how formidable becomes the task of coping with the complexities of industrial society – the machine which strives to fit them all together! As Gordon Rattray Taylor writes: '. . . our society, when it presents people with challenges, tends to present them with impossibly difficult ones or ones which are too easy.' There is no slot for us. We acquire a growing feeling that we are surrounded by situations with which we cannot cope. We strive to achieve something, only to find that remote decision-makers – whether

politicians, planners, employers or shop stewards – can smother our efforts in an instant. There is an air of impermanence; we feel that change is overtaking us too rapidly; we become alienated, and only too ready to let experts take control. In short we become conditioned to accept what is around us: we cease to question, and therein lies a grave danger.

One survivalist I met on my travels was Kit Pedler, best known as author of the TV series 'Doomwatch' and science fiction writer; less well known as possessor of two doctorates, as a pathologist and biologist, and as an author of a different kind, with thirty-eight papers on the eye and vision – the result of 12 years' intense specialisation.

When I visited him, at his London, Clapham, home, he was working on plans for making old and new houses as autonomous as possible, and vehement on the danger of human conditioning. 'Technical man,' he said, 'is totally conditioned to accept the artifacts from a great industrial complex, without any regard for the consequences to all – globally or environmentally. He still thinks that as long as there are Concordes, deep-freezes and ten different varieties of frozen peas, with the enormous and totally mendacious commercialisation that goes with them to induce him to buy them, all is well. He is totally conditioned to accept it all. Technical man, particularly in the cities, has never been shown the effect of all those things on the earth around him. He sees a new factory going up, and he thinks "Great – that means more employment for more people". He omits to realise, to quote just one side-effect, that the area covered by the factory is an area of potential agricultural land gone forever. He doesn't see the full circle, because he has never been educated to think this way. Everything around him in the commercial world, where he lives, teaches him that all this growth is good and produces civility for him.

'In fact it is a short-term thing which is already collapsing from the inside, but he is not allowed to hear this. The forces of large industrial and political organisations teach him that all is well, when it manifestly isn't. In a cash-based society we only recognise changes in costs, so that economists talk about "inflation". But what is really happening is that the earth is becoming like a wrinkled apple and drying up.

'*Of course* resources are rising in cost – they're harder to find. It's no good believing the economists and thinking all will be well if we make some more money or buy some more money or some half-intelligent thing like that. The last thing I'd like in my bank is money. You can't eat it, you can't take it to bed, build houses with it . . .

'It's a terrible conditioning system. There's no board of evil managing directors doing it, no one man at the top saying "Right, we've got to keep these people quiet". It just happens. The profit motive is at the root of it. Your top industrialists bent on profit – they are the victims as well, pathetic creatures who have to work to keep the system going. They would like the alternative but they don't know how to do it, because they're as conditioned as anyone else – they're just richer.'

During my travels I was to hear a variation on the same theme from others: at Berkeley University for instance, Sim van Der Ryn, an American architect, had discovered that being one had nothing to do with building.

Sitting with me in the warm Californian sun, beside University buildings – so hideous, so inhumane that teachers like him found they could no longer teach in them – he explained how people in American cities had become conditioned to accept 'urban impotence' – a way of life that lulled them into becoming increasingly dependent on institutions and experts. 'A housewife can't even put up a shelf,' he lamented, 'and the older people get, the less confidence they have to do anything at all with their hands.' He told me how he had tried to break down this brand of alienation by helping people build their own homes. 'As soon as people get involved in making something, it just catches hold,' he enthused. 'Like what's happened with foods: a home you've made yourself is like home-baked bread is to bought bread. It's all part of a need people have to create more of the substances of their lives.' In America, as in Britain, it seemed that building codes aided the alienation process. 'They make having a home unnecessarily expensive,' he claimed. 'They've been used to persecute people and I've been active in trying to get them changed. Once you begin to *rethink* your life, then you quickly find out that what's provided has a whole lot of built-in values you can't accept.'

As I talked with such people I came to see that a conditioned society in which people feel alienated and impotent is an inhospitable climate for love to flourish; and the dearth of love is manifested in other ways, not least by lack of concern for the rest of life on earth – for the very planet itself. Once this impoverishment is appreciated, it becomes easier to understand the unconcern of rich countries for the plight of the Third World, the relentless extinction of other species, and the wholesale violation of the biosphere. We can begin to see how we have turned away from the mystery of life to the mastery of things.

Alternative Technology
The imposed society is not blind to its imperfections, and from time to time it makes – or promises to make – attempts to correct them. Pollution is a prime example.

In the role of Britain's Tory Prime Minister, Edward Heath in 1974 urged more industrial activity as the way, not only to personal happiness, but also – oddly enough – to combat the very pollution which industrial growth produces. He proclaimed: '. . . the struggle against pollution requires massive resources which can only come from the economic expansion.' Later in the year, when Labour had ousted the Tory Government, its Secretary of State for the Environment, Anthony Crosland, dwelt on the cost of coping with pollution. 'We have no chance of funding these huge sums from a near static GNP,' he declared. 'Only rapid growth would give us any possibility.'

Similar opinions, echoed by others, from Lord Zuckerman, former Chief Government Scientist, to experts of the World Bank, reflect the solidarity behind the conviction that more technology is needed to clean up the mess created by technology.

They also throw into sharp relief the dichotomy between conventional wisdom and the survivalists' U-turn approach.

This eccentric minority sees most of us as sick – distracted into a pursuit of materialism which will destroy us and quite possibly the biosphere along with us. The cure, they say, lies not in trying to satisfy an insatiable appetite, but in *reducing* it, so that we begin to live as we once did – more in accord with nature. Many dissenters, however, have not yet thought things through to this stage. 'Never mind the future,' they say, 'it's the present that matters.'

They find themselves incapable of accepting either the present as it is or the promises that it will soon get better. They object to doing boring, pointless work. Education seems irrelevant. They abhor the violence and squalor which are part of the urban scene. They resent the corruption and cynicism condoned in government and business institutions. They are sickened by the apathy and dual moral standards of people everywhere. They feel helpless, and any attempt they may make to put things right within the system only seems to prop it up. In consequence they feel empty, confused, lonely and unfulfilled. There must, they believe, be something better.

The two groups have much in common. Basically they seek a different way of living which demands less instead of exploiting more. They aim to reverse the exodus to the cities by setting viable rural communities, while within the cities they are trying to re-establish a sense of local community. They hope to revive variety in the place of uniformity and to reinstate the satisfaction that work can give. And they seek a feeling of control over their destinies.

The dissenters are not saying that science and technology are wrong and we must all turn mediaeval. Far from it. They believe that the benefits of science should be redirected to serve true human needs and create a society based on sound ecological principles.

The concept of redirecting science and technology comes in a variety of names: 'alternative technology' is perhaps the best known; 'intermediate', 'soft', 'socially appropriate', 'utopian', 'biotechnic', and 'low impact technology' are others. In practice they all amount to using our knowledge, skills and resources to solve the important human and ecological problems rather than squander them on esoteric ones: problems on which to focus include ignorance, poverty, hunger, disease, unemployment, urban decay, alienation, boredom, environmental abuses, pollution, the energy crisis, and the concentration of political and economic power in the hands of those who are already powerful.

Alternative technology takes many forms. It means using the sun, wind, rivers and tides for power. It is a new kind of architecture which makes use of local, renewable materials – and sometimes waste products. It means living in a way that reduces the input of non-renewable materials and re-uses waste products as a source of power, as fertiliser and as building materials. It aims to grow food without spraying poisons. Alternative communication media are encouraged, spawning small, often local, independent periodicals and radio stations to inform and involve. Workers and local communities share in the control and ownership of their industrial enterprises. Organisations are kept small or divided into manageable units. More things are made by satisfying craftsmanship rather than mass production. In fact the whole concept implies a shift from making *products* towards serving *people* – whether this involves products or not. And so we find more preventive medicine and dentistry; education which aims to raise awareness rather than pump in facts; industry based on labour-intensive rather than capital-intensive methods; more walking and cycling, less movement for movement's sake. But alternative technology and its attendant life-styles add up to far more than a freakish, back-to-the-soil, do-it-yourself religious revival, strictly for cultists. Their practitioners claim they have a genuine relevance to today.

They are united, however loosely, by seeking alternative choices, which lie outside the mainstream of the imposed society. They claim no monopoly in wanting a better society, nor in living life according to their tastes and dreams. Their uniqueness, if any, is their recognition of a fundamental sickness in industrial society which simply cannot be cured by 'more of the same'. Some believe that the change they seek can be accomplished politically by a conventional shift to the Left, but for a political solution a greater number look to some form of anarchy as the only way of meeting the prime need for decentralisation. Others admit to having lost faith and interest in politics as a weapon for change, even though a political shift must take place after change.

For them the emphasis is on individual action – the 'demonstration effect' of acting out your beliefs rather than preaching about them. 'You can't change the mass,' they say, 'you can only change, even though a political shift must take place after their beliefs into practice the ripple effect could be dramatic. Some of them, however, see the technology of mass communications as their ally: if a pop tune or a fashion in clothes can encompass the world within weeks, why not truth? For them the change is spiritual first, political second.

Robin Clarke caught the spirit of the movement when he wrote: '. . . men before machines, people before governments, practice before theory, student before teacher, country before the city, smallness before bigness, wholeness before reductionism, organic materials before synthetic ones, plants before animals, craftsmanship before expertise, and quality before quantity.'

Scratch a survivalist in any Western nation and you will probably find some infection from the counter culture, the original, youthful opposition to the technocratic society. In the manner of the early Christians, they carried the torch of protest flaming into our own times, challenging almost all that the society of our time holds most dear: its modernising, rationalising, planning, efficiency, large-scale organisation, competition, activity and progress. They revived visionary experience; declared feeling to be more vital than knowing; unleashed spontaniety and sensuality. They de-trivialised sex, re-asserted love and community, revitalised politics and subordinated technical expertise. If they achieved less than their dreams and visions proclaimed, their failure was more because the society they threatened digested and commercialised their songs, their dreams, drugs and artifacts than because they failed to express the human needs which the society was busily stifling.

This youthful opposition was the precursor to ecological awakening and the subsequent growth of alternative technology. If youth focused more on immediate personal experience than long-term survival, it was because the early prophets of the environmental movement had not yet been heeded and the dimensions of their predictions smacked of guesses and remoteness; moreover world poverty had not yet been exposed as relevant, threatening or worthy of more than handouts. The counter culture was right for its time, for it sensitised the imposed society to contemplate the next act in the drama of survival which was soon to follow.

Survivalists act in various ways. Some escape to remote places. Alone or in groups, they 'want out'. In doing so they may seek to rediscover lost love within their intentional communities; they may also seek to minimise their harm to the planet by living closer to nature, reducing their wants and eschewing waste. Some, on the other hand, elect to stay within the imposed society to recreate there a new structure of values, so that needs take priority over wants, and people begin to care more for people than for things. Some of them seek to re-awaken within cities an awareness of a city's dependence on the countryside beyond, so that its citizens may look on it as more than a cross between playground and food factory. Others are turning their attention to the Third World where the life-supporting needs of food and shelter are most widely lacking. This brand of survivalists tends to see world poverty, not as some historical or geographical accident, but in cold, clear terms of rich exploiting poor: by manipulating world currency agreements and trade terms, and at the same time by exporting inappropriate technologies. In a world of limited resources our fruitless attempts in rich nations to satisfy wants are preventing our fellow humans in poor nations from satisfying their needs.

The Other Two Billion

Harold Dickinson is a plump, energetic and outspoken university lecturer who fights untiringly in the cause of survival. An ardent admirer of China and a caustic battler for the world's two billion under-privileged, he lives and works in Edinburgh, but tends to be elusive. Word has got around among the two billion that he has two outstanding assets: he knows and he cares. In contrast to some experts from government departments or multinational companies, he has nothing to sell. Any Third World country, which invites him to fly out and advise on an irrigation scheme or community factory, can be assured that it has not issued an invitation to be sold inappropriate technology. Harold Dickinson understands what the district will want; as an engineer he knows not only the technologies available, but the means to create ones which will be appropriate to it. And if anyone doubts whether he cares about the people who pay scarce cash to secure his services, they should try debating with him the subject of world poverty and its perpetrators. 'We can't pull out,' he says of the Western powers. 'We've already intervened: the missionary days of gin and colonial forces disrupted society in Africa and elsewhere; then just when they were getting over the shock, we in the rich countries invented DDT and gave them a population problem. Then having got around to looking at the problems this created, we educate the young of these countries to come here and solve *our* problems – and leave theirs alone. That's why now we must take care to decide whether *any* action is socially appropriate. I don't see development without social change – change that is right for each place where it happens. But if developing countries insist on following the road that is leading *us* to disaster, I'm sure it will lead them to disaster as well. Remember, peasant societies in Africa have been sustained for up to 10,000 years by their own technologies; ours have sustained us for only a hundred, and we realise now that it all can't go on much longer. They've got stability and we've a lot to learn from them.'

Harold Dickinson identifies three main kinds of worriers about the future: those concerned with finding and applying appropriate technologies with which the developing nations can help their people survive; ecologists concerned with what industrial society is doing to the biosphere; and 'latterday worriers' in industry, who have suddenly discovered that the flows of energy and raw materials upon which they have built their societies are showing signs of strain. When this group explores alternative ways to maintain the flow, they run contrary to the beliefs of the ecologists; moreover, the flow can be maintained only at the expense of the poor countries of the world. So there is friction. But this is not all, for the 'appropriate developers' and the ecologists also tend to look at each other with antagonism: the developers want to use energy sources to provide minimal development possibilities, using intermediate, appropriate technology; but the ecologists maintain that this will only create *more* pollution from *more* industry of the same old exploitive kind.

'These threads must be drawn together, to achieve some meaningful solution,' he insists. 'There are limits to the total amount of energy that you can dissipate into the biosphere, but no one knows what that limit is. So far all the research and development has looked at the wrong side of the problem.'

The 'energy crisis' has provoked a sudden realisation that middle-class attitudes to possessions and waste are not universal, and may possibly be terminal, he says. With a hardening of attitudes towards poor countries, the immediate reaction of the rich is to gain control of the remaining resources rather than share them rationally. It is generally recognised that the world now has an energy crisis, a resource crisis, a population crisis, a food crisis, and a pollution crisis – all because of the ephemeral demand of a small number of members of the human race.

Harold Dickinson, however, sees the paramount crisis differently from most other survivalists: he calls it 'a sink crisis'. On this he is emphatic: 'The determining parameter is not what we take from the world, but what we put into the biosphere.' The science and art of maintaining this critical balance he terms 'equilibrium technology'. It is this which should decide our technologies, he declares: they must offer attainable expectations to the increasingly politically conscious poor of the world; they must be socially appropriate for each place; but above all they must conform to the ecological requirements of the biosphere – which he irreverently terms 'the sink'. In other words: we neglect the needs of the biosphere at our peril.

Harold Dickinson neither underestimates man's ingenuity nor the rich minority's determination to take all it can get at the expense of the poor, whatever the consequent global strife. Yet even this chilling prospect takes second place to the effect on the biosphere of ever increasing energy consumption. One factor is inescapable: all energy conversion ultimately leads to thermal pollution – heating up 'the sink'. If the rate at which pollution is increasing exceeds the capacity of 'the sink' to absorb or lose it, thermal equilibrium will have been lost and may never be regained. Man will have flagrantly violated one of the biosphere's prime needs.

So far we have been lucky: the rise in temperature of the world shows no signs of destroying the biosphere, although there is direct evidence that local effects may have global consequences. 'As yet man's intervention is not known to have had repercussions on the scale of natural disasters, but,' he warns, 'irreversible large scale ecological changes may have already been triggered.'

Chapter Three:
The energy illusion

The mantle of life which we call the biosphere is, as we have seen, a system in which normally everything is re-used in a way which makes it richer, more diverse and sustainable. Several million years ago, however, long before the advent of man, the system developed a fault. Some of the dead material – plant and animal debris – slipped out of sight, deep into the earth's crust, even as deep as 13,000 feet. Down there it promised to be lost to the system forever, for no sunlight could reach it, no roots or micro-organisms could raise it to the surface and back to the system from which it had escaped. It had died, and fossilised it promised to remain – a mistake of no great consequence apparently, for it happened at a time of unparalleled abundance in the earth's long history of fertility, and, even though it amounted to billions of tons of organic matter, life above thrived unabatedly.

Some of the lost fossilised material was solid, plant debris crushed and trapped in long seams; some of it was liquid, the remains of marine creatures, filtered under pressure into porous rock; and some of this liquid changed under extreme conditions of heat and pressure into gas.

Now, however, the full consequences of this 'mistake' are being revealed, for in the last two hundred years man has applied himself with ever-increasing vigour to the task of returning the lost material to the system – as coal, oil, and natural gas. This fossil fuel made possible the industrial revolution which made possible the mass exploitation of every potentially usable resource of the planet. No longer did man have to rely for energy on mere wind, water, and muscle power, whether animal or human, all of them puny and unpredictable. Now, for the first time, he possessed, so it seemed, unlimited energy, conveniently packaged to be shipped wherever it was needed.

Not until a decade or two ago did his consciousness embrace either the prospect that such abundance might dry up or that its use could have seriously harmful side-effects. He never envisaged the catastrophic population explosion that would follow in its wake. It had not occurred to him that thermal pollution could endanger the atmosphere or the stability of the polar ice caps, or that poisons, made possible by abundant energy, could threaten the food chains. It did not occur to him that it would sharply divide the peoples of the earth: that those who had the use of energy and the resources to which it gave them access would grow rich at the expense of those who were denied them, or that, in the course of time, such a split would put him under the constant shadow of nuclear war – itself a direct consequence of the original discovery; and it never dawned on him that those with access to this cheap, convenient energy would become so dependent on it – in the manner of a dangerous drug – that, to avoid withdrawal symptoms, they would risk the extinction, not only of their own species, but of the entire biosphere. For the only 'feasible' alternative energy source to fossil fuel yet known is nuclear power, a force outside of nature and – in the hands of a creature as arrogant and immature as man – so potentially destructive that it is both beyond the capacity of most of us to contemplate and inconvenient for profiteers to publicise.

The blunt truth is now starkly revealed. When man accidentally discovered, less than two hundred years ago, the abundance of this accidental loss from the biosphere of several million years ago, he inherited the power to destroy *all* life within a matter of decades. And he wasted little time in perfecting the means!

It is this prospect which has set a small minority seeking alternatives which offer a better chance for the survival of all life forms.

The conventional approach to the problem of an energy

shortage is to make every effort to maintain business as usual: to make belated attempts at reducing the blatant wastage of energy; to offer bigger bribes to men that they should risk their lives digging coal; to lay waste the land with open-cast coal mining; to spend ever more heavily on the search for more oil; to exploit marginal reserves, such as oil shale sands and deep ocean deposits, which pose inadmissible environmental hazards and degradation; to invest in highly centralised and large-scale alternative sources, such as geothermal energy, conventional hydro-electricity, tidal power, solar energy, and nuclear power.

The approach of the survivalists is different. Firstly, they say that we must all recognise that energy is the only finite resource that cannot be recycled: when a ton of oil has been burned, it has gone for ever. Secondly, they say we must recognise that energy is the mainspring of all industrial activity which supports life, as well as that which entertains us. And thirdly they stress that its use, even at the present level, must not jeopardise life, either born or yet to be born. If these premises are accepted we have to think again about the kind of energy we use and what we use it for. The world's affluent minority must learn to be happy with less – as most of the world have to do already. Not only must we curb our appetite for energy, but we must look for non-polluting, renewable alternatives that exploit neither mankind nor the planet.

The survivalists have few allies among the Establishment. Occasionally, a lone scientist, politician or industrialist steps out of line and makes headlines, but he is promptly forgotten. In July 1974 an impressive working party representing the Institute of Fuel, the Royal Society of Arts, and the Committee for Environmental Conservation (which represents all the major conservation organisations) achieved brief mention when it published an important report, *Energy and the Environment*. Written by high-level technical specialists, balanced by laymen experienced in social and environmental matters, the report focused its grave concern on the likely consequences of any 'crash programme' for nuclear power, with special emphasis on fast-breeder reactors:

'The only foreseeable means by which the projected commitment to fast-breeder reactors can be postponed appears to be by control of energy demand,' the report stated. It foresaw a serious nuclear accident from conventional nuclear power stations somewhere in the world during the next 25 years, 'particularly as the care of these installations passes to less skilled and dedicated men'. And it added that the fate of nuclear installations and stored waste during war or civil unrest and the vulnerability to sabotage also warranted concern.

Around the same time the British Government unveiled its plans for a major programme of electricity generated from extra nuclear power stations!

Energy direct from the Sun
Except for nuclear and geothermal energy, all the energy we use – or could use – comes from the sun, and throughout history we have concentrated our efforts into tapping this energy indirectly rather than directly. The food which fuels our bodies, fossil fuels, hydro-electric power, wind and water power are nothing more than second-hand solar energy. Because indirect solar energy has been cheap and abundant, direct use of the sun's rays has been left to a few enthusiasts, virtually ignored by the rest of the world. Almost overnight however the picture has changed. In the cool northern latitudes of the USA, Europe, the USSR and Japan, where industrial activity is greatest and fossil fuel dependence consequently highest, people are at last taking note that, although they may flock south for sunshine holidays, their homes, factories and land are literally bombarded by free solar energy running to waste.

This energy can never replace fossil fuel as the mainspring of industrial output, nor for heating homes in large cities; but it can be used to supplement conventional energy supplies and so help to make dwindling fuel stocks last longer. In sunny rural districts where people live far apart and electricity distribution costs are disproportionate, its potential is even greater. Moreover, it can help to make country people less dependent on cities and so encourage decentralisation.

In Third World countries, the direct use of the sun's energy has a vast liberating potential. As the developed world has learned to its cost, a small number of developing countries already possess the oil reserves upon which it became dependent; the majority of Third World countries however lack adequate energy sources ... apart from sunshine, and it is here that they are extra fortunate. For example the vast, dust-free desert area of north Chile, which has 364 sunny days and one millimetre of rain a year, theoretically receives more solar heat than all the heat produced in the world from conventional fuels. Anthony Tucker, science correspondent of the *Guardian*, has pointed out that, although, for example, mainland Africa, excluding the Middle East, has less than one-tenth of the estimated coal reserves of the US and less than one-third of the oil reserves of the Middle East, its solar input is enormous and remarkably uniform throughout the year: solar power there could be used for about ten hours a day all the year round.

'The enormous advantage of sunlight is that it is distributed free, and properly used in developing areas, could prevent the disastrous concentration of population in urban areas, through drift from the land,' he writes. 'The kind of energy systems being thrust on to developing areas or being chosen by them for questionable reasons – such as nuclear reactors – require large-scale grid systems and inevitably lead to urban conglomeration.'

If, over the years, a small fraction of the research and development lavished on exploring and exploiting fossil fuel and nuclear power had been diverted to improving ways of using the sun's energy direct, many of the two billion people still without electricity for heating, lighting, or pumping water would have their basic needs better satisfied. The neglect of this free, non-polluting energy source is a classic example of technology misapplied in the pursuit of greed.

Solar energy is versatile. It will heat or cool whole houses, provide hot water, run refrigerators, bake and boil food, help generate methane gas, distill fresh water from salt water, heat fish-farm ponds, dry farm produce, pump water, run engines, and power potters' kilns and small industrial furnaces. Coupled to high technology it will even generate electricity direct via a fuel cell, and, although this has so far proved uneconomic, new developments in this field could change the picture.

Solar energy can be concentrated by using a lens, or more commonly a reflector, but to do so the equipment must be mounted so as to follow the sun throughout the day. A more common apparatus is the stationary flat plate collector. Designs vary, but it is basically a shallow air-tight box, mounted so as to face the sun for as much of the day as possible. Near the bottom of the box is a plate of sheet metal – usually copper, aluminium or iron – which is blackened for maximum heat absorption. Above this, forming the top of the box, are one or two sheets of glass or clear plastic. These create a greenhouse effect, trapping the heat from the long-wavelengths of solar energy and reducing radiation losses. Either over or under the blackened sheet, and close to it, a fluid circulates, usually by means of a pump. This fluid – commonly water with anti-freeze added – absorbs the heat from the hot plate and transfers it to an insulated water storage tank. The hot water can be used for a domestic hot water system, or for space heating, either with central heating radiators or a convector fan blowing air over hot water pipes.

In Britain the commonest use of solar energy is to pre-heat water so as to reduce the consumption of electricity or other energy sources. However, every country and every district within a country has its peculiarities of climate, its own local materials and labour with which to make the equipment to collect this energy and convert it to usable power. One survivalist who keeps this principle well in mind is a Canadian – Tom Lawand, director of the Brace Research Institute. There in Quebec he motivates a tiny staff who have pioneered work in alternative technology for the Third World for over a decade.

When I met him, I soon sensed the energy and dedication which has given the Institute a world-wide reputation and effec tiveness out of all proportion to its size. 'We're finding solutions to the problems faced by the hundreds of millions of people outside the main stream of development whose everyday lives aren't affected by the achievements of modern technology,' he told me. 'In all our work we make use of whatever may be locally available; we adapt the technology so that the villager feels part of the work and its results. He helps to make the equipment, he runs it when we've moved on, and he enjoys the benefits of it. Too often in development, human dignity is left out of the equation. Whatever we do, we're guided by the principle that the final proof and justification of it is whether or not it's acceptable to ordinary people.

'In Haiti, with money from Oxfam, we helped a small country community build a solar distillation plant which we'd designed. Since we left 4 years ago the people there have been running it. With pure fresh water their health has improved and the local economy has picked up. In Haiti too we installed solar cookers for schoolchildren's midday meal, and later distributed a number of small ones to communities and individuals – having cut down most of their trees, Haitians have a real fuel problem.'

Tom Lawand makes full use of the staff and facilities of the Faculty of Engineering in McGill University, where he is based, but Lawand-inspired installations are scattered throughout the Third World, from the Caribbean to Africa. Although the Institute also researches into wind power, it specialises in water desalination and solar stills, and, with a growing interest in arid areas, it has extended its work to research in how to grow crops with less water. In Turkey, for example, solar stills are being used in conjunction with greenhouses as a way of conserving fresh water. Apart from this, the Institute has developed low-cost, family-sized, solar-energy-powered devices for heating water and drying crops; it has also developed farm-sized crop dryers, as well as a ten-horse power low-cost turbine run from solar steam power. Tom Lawand, moreover, is no believer in keeping findings locked up, and the Institute publishes and disseminates do-it-yourself booklets so that appropriate technologies can be applied to any part of the world.

Although he is deeply concerned with the problems of overseas countries, he does not neglect Canada; the Institute also works on the problems of a country with isolated communities and climatic extremes. 'Canada is an undeveloped country,' he told me. 'Sure we've prosperous cities, but out in the rural areas there are people living in conditions no better than many parts of the Third World. They're forgotten people who need help badly.'

Another country with an interest in solar energy is Australia. The International Solar Energy Society moved its headquarters from Arizona to Melbourne in 1970, and it was there, in 1973, at a symposium of the society that R. N. Morse, chief of CSIRO Division of Mechanical Engineering, predicted that, by the year 2000, solar energy could supply a quarter of Australia's primary energy. This would require substantial research, development, and industrial effort, he stressed – unlikely, however, in view of the country's big coal reserves.

He foresaw half of Australia's solar energy potential as coming indirectly – by processing trees and plants to produce synthetic liquid and gaseous fuel, to take the place of fossil fuel supplies as they ran out. He found such a prospect attractive: 'Our population density and the nature of our land resources are such that it could supply us with a solution to our energy problems which is not available to other countries, if a few per cent of our land could provide our liquid and gaseous fuels in perpetuity.'

On this point he showed signs of parting company with the survivalists, for he saw this fuel principally as a way to keep the country's transportation system running. A survivalist, in contrast, would prefer a policy of decentralisation which would *reduce* fuel requirements. The concept of feeding vehicles with farm and forest produce in preference to feeding *people* from the same land has a ring of dubious morality. It implies the unlikely prediction that one favoured country could carry on as before, while the rest of the world goes under.

I asked F. G. Hogg, Secretary of the Australia and New Zealand

Section of the International Solar Energy Society, just how much use Australia was making of solar energy, and he replied that, apart from a few solar stills, its only use – a growing one – was for heating domestic water. 'The picture may change over the years,' he said, 'but we have no shortage of coal, or natural gas, and we are virtually self-sufficient in petroleum products. In other words we have no energy crisis.'

Power from the Wind

Wind power is one of the oldest energy sources known to man, still a vital source for millions of people as yet unblessed by high technology, and now a source of renewed interest among those who are. Wind power's first uses were to grind grain and pump water – for irrigation, livestock, or household water – and in Third World countries these are still its chief uses. Now, however, as electricity costs soar and blackouts or brownouts become more frequent, wind generators are being sought and built in growing numbers throughout the industrialised nations. In Canada, for example, two scientists with the National Research Council have designed a wind generator which costs around £20 and can deliver one kilowatt in a mere 15 m.p.h. wind. And the Canadian Government is interested in building a 30-foot high unit to power and heat remote houses in districts even as cold as the Arctic. But research in Canada has not been confined to small-scale schemes. Two scientists, Dick Bell and Glen Hook, in British Columbia, have calculated that all the electrical energy needed by the 1969 population of the province could have been generated by 893 wind generators with 200-feet-diameter blades; 1969 is the last year for which per capita energy consumption figures are available, and to cater for present and future needs the number of generators would be somewhat greater. The generators could be sited on the Queen Charlotte Islands where the wind blows strongly for 99 per cent of the time. This exceptional consistency would reduce the storage problems usually inherent in wind-powered generation. Normally wind-powered generators suffer from the same disadvantage as solar power: the energy source is intermittent and even less predictable. This means that some way of storing their electricity must be found: in batteries; by compressing air, or by pumping water to uphill storage, in each case to generate electricity when required; or as kinetic energy in the form of a flywheel. None of these methods is either cheap or particularly efficient, but there is a fascination about 'free' wind power, and interest in it is unabated: among survivalists seeking freedom from the system or working on Third World development, among genuine experimenters seeking more efficient power sources for sparsely populated districts than the electricity grid, and among the trendy rich seeking a new conversation piece.

Wind-powered generators come in all sizes. Depending on how windy your site is, the height of your tower, and the size and design of your propeller unit, you can expect to generate anything from 100 to 1,000 watts *when the wind blows*. On my travels I encountered most sizes – from the smallest in action to one of the largest projected. The smallest I saw was at the New Alchemy Institute at Woods Hole, Massachusetts, where Dr John Todd leads a team of survivalists dedicated 'to restore the lands, protect the seas, and inform the earth's stewards'. There a bicycle wheel had been modified by securing propeller blades to the spokes – the wheel mounted on a pole so that it would remain facing the wind. In its hub was a Sturmey-Archer 'Dynohub' generator, from which wires had been led to a trickle-charger feeding a six-volt battery. After a day's charging from a fair breeze, the one or two watts output from this modest device would light a lamp or run a radio for an evening.

I encountered the other extreme at Brunel University, just west of London, where a staff of 700 process some 1,800 undergraduates for entry into the imposed society.

One of the 700 is Jack Parsons, sociologist with a strong interest in energy problems. It was he who, in 1973, convened a handful of students and staff into the Brunel Environment Group 'to foster care and good husbandry of the resources entrusted to us by society'; and it was he who encouraged two initial projects alien to the conventions of the imposed society. One project is a student-built autonomous house, independent from outside services for heat, light, water, and sewage treatment; the other a wind generator big enough to free the campus from complete dependence on the electricity grid. With untiring energy and infectious enthusiasm, Jack Parsons has skilfully steered both projects through the maze of university bureaucracy and inter-departmental jealousies. They are both his children, yet of the two the wind-power generator most seizes his imagination.

He was concerned about ecology, about man's affairs and the state of the world long before the energy crisis, he admits, but it has been the University's rapacious energy appetite which has changed his concern into action. Its widely scattered glass and concrete buildings might almost have been specially designed to consume maximum energy, and this set him searching for a non-polluting, renewable alternative. A spot of research revealed that a 1·25 megawatt wind generator had been built in Vermont during the war and had operated satisfactorily until 1945. Around 1950 a 3·6 megawatt monster was designed for the Orkneys, but, although feasible, it was never built. Since then he has discovered that over the years the USSR has built scores of wind generators in a range of sizes.

Jack Parsons and his group looked into Brunel's power require-ments and searched through the somewhat inadequate records to see how strong the wind blew across its site. They found that the average wind velocity at ground level was a mere 10 m.p.h. – a fraction of the Orkneys' 35 m.p.h. – but, at a height of 250 feet, it could rise to 15 m.p.h. – encouraging, since wind energy rises with the cube of the velocity. They did some sums and found that if they built a wind generator on top of a 250-foot tower, with a propeller up to 225 feet in diameter, even with this wind velocity it could generate up to 350 kilowatts. If they could only find a way of storing surplus energy to tide them over calm days this output could supply perhaps a third of the University's needs – an even higher proportion if its appetite were tamed. And with its

1974 electricity bill expected to touch £126,000, the challenge was inspiring.

There were snags of course, and not the least was construction cost. To put the work out to contract would probably be prohibitive, but an answer was at hand: a do-it-yourself job! As Jack Parsons explains: 'We could design the thing and fabricate it in our own workshops as part of the educational process, steering towards the windmill project funds which are already being spent on materials and processes for student projects and the like. So we'd be spending the same amount of money making windmill parts instead of things to be thrown on the scrap heap. In fact, if we built a number of functions – radio and TV transmitters and receivers, tutorial rooms and so on – into one tall, thin building strong enough to take a windmill on top, we could even make a profit on the deal!'

The group considered two ways of dealing with the problem of storing any surplus power, and one was to sell it to the Central Electricity Generating Board by feeding it into the grid; but the alternative which Jack Parsons fancied was to store it on the campus. New kinds of batteries would be one solution to the formidable technical problem of storage, but he preferred to explore the possibility of kinetic storage with a 225-ton underground flywheel rotating at 3,500 r.p.m. and capable of storing 10,000 killowatt hours. Wind-powered electricity would keep the wheel spinning until calm periods, when its colossal momentum would be used to drive the generators until the wind got up again.

For a while Jack Parsons was the campus's lone wind freak, but once his ideas appeared in the University news-letter, interest and enthusiasm grew, while from outside the University offers of practical help and advice began to flow in – as well as the prospect of a useful grant of money. Much of the advice was encouraging, but opposition began to develop among some of the engineers: 'We may have to content ourselves with a much smaller experimental structure of, say, 30 feet radius,' he admitted. In any event, there would first of all have to be a feasibility study – for which he was seeking funds – to learn if the campus site would be economic; if it proved not to be, the generator would have to be sited near enough to use the power; but if neither were economic it would have to be built somewhere quite unrelated to Brunel – defeating the main object, but still providing something useful for the wider society. The answer is blowin' in the wind . . .

When I saw him on the campus, I asked him what he, a sociologist, was doing dabbling in wind generators and 'eco-houses'. 'I don't regard myself as a very good or a proper sociologist,' he answered, 'more a Jack of all Trades. I think sociologists in particular, and social scientists in general, should take more notice of "environmental imperatives". Social systems which ignore the "absolutes" in the physical environment perish – they go under. There are resource constraints on social systems and I argue this in my courses here; and I argue with my colleagues that their own teaching ought to be ecologically informed.'

If Jack Parsons gets his windmill built and working, will it represent a solution which is compatible with the needs of man and the biosphere? On balance the answer is probably 'no'. A survivalist would argue forcibly, firstly against building a monstrosity such as a large, energy-hungry university in the first place. He would question the need for a huge centralised information factory, producing assembly-line human products, groomed for the industrialised, imposed society. He would inquire whether a windmill on the same scale was not part of the fatal syndrome of 'more technology to cure the problems generated by misapplied technology'. He would ask whether the things, which Jack Parsons says are made by students and thrown on the scrap heap, could not instead become things made to help satisfy the needs of the poor; or if this were not possible he would ask if they could simply be recycled. And he might suggest that, if society *must* continue to bear the social cost of maintaining the campus, the students might perhaps more profitably devote their thoughts and skills to insulating the buildings and generally applying themselves to reducing the energy appetite of the place they occupy.

Neglected Water Power

Water power is probably man's oldest source of energy. Grinding corn and pumping water were long, laborious tasks which no doubt gave him ample time to think of ways to replace human and animal muscle-power. The waterwheel almost certainly dates back to 100 years before the birth of Christ; in the Britain of 1066, 8,000 watermills provided power for fewer than a million people, and if each delivered a likely two-and-a-half horsepower the average energy available to each person would have been a constant and useful one-fifth of a horsepower or more. Around this time the feudal lords of the manor began preventing their tenants from building their own mills – and compelled them to grind their corn at the manorial mills – a useful source of income. And if a tenant bent on self-sufficiency used even a handmill in his own home he was liable to punishment.

Here indeed were the seeds of a continuing policy of power centralisation, which in this century has led to the abandonment of small, individually operated power sources and their replacement by huge inefficient schemes. Hydro-electric schemes are ecologically harmful and dams quickly silt up. Power stations, whether coal, oil or nuclear powered, deliberately waste two-thirds of their energy in generating unused heat; and, when distribution and other losses are included, finally deliver only some ten per cent of the original energy to the unfortunate consumer! As the whole creaking edifice of centralised power distribution becomes increasingly vulnerable – to threats from foreign oil producers, to industrial unrest, sabotage and accident – the pendulum is beginning to swing back, and the small streams, which until last century boasted at least one waterwheel for every village and hamlet, are a focus of renewed interest.

This is specially so in the USA, where a back-to-the-land movement is well under way and the potential of the small stream has captured the imagination of a multitude of survivalists and attendant gadget-happy do-it-yourself freaks. As if they had just invented the wheel, they are discovering that they can make their own electricity and pump their own water, either continuously or in emergency; and that the pond which is often created raises fish for sport or as a crop. In Britain too there is renewed interest in small-scale water power, but anyone with ideas of self-sufficiency will soon find himself in the clutches of bureaucracy.

Throughout much of the Third World, lack of water ranks equal with lack of food as the number one problem for people in remote areas, where small-scale water power is essential for tasks such as grinding grain, pumping drinking water for people and for livestock, and irrigating crops. In affluent countries, governments and industrialists alike pour money and energy into selling these countries glamorous, high technology projects such as big hydro-electric schemes and nuclear power stations – the spin-off from their own industrial output. In contrast, alongside them a handful of survivalists are working on a shoestring, peddling the idea of locally appropriate, small-scale water schemes to provide power and other basic needs. In Britain, for example, George McCrobie runs the Intermediate Technology Development Group, which subsists on a tiny budget, working with universities, industry and aid organisations such as Oxfam and Christian Aid to research and sponsor small-scale local industries. One of his projects has been to study the effects of water supplies on village life. This has found that villagers are prevented from growing all the food they need, not only from lack of water, but because of the time they spend in simply *getting to it*: villagers – usually women – spend hours a day carrying water on foot, while their horses, donkeys and oxen waste much of their working day simply walking to the local dam or stream to drink. Clearly, simple pumping devices and piping would transform the villagers' lives, and George McCrobie and his team are trying to get schemes for water and wind power under way. Meanwhile in the USA the Volunteers for International Technical Assistance (VITA) does similar work. One of its members, Hans W. Hamm, has made a special study of the needs of such people, and his handbook, *Low Cost Development of Small Water-power Sites*, is a little classic. In it, a detailed questionnaire has been designed to help a VITA engineer to plan a small water-power site for a community or an individual. In comparison with the activities of the multinational companies, exporting their technologies to the Third World with an eye to expanding markets, the efforts of ITDG, VITA and other voluntary agencies appear puny. In their own countries they encounter apathy, opposition, and even ridicule; in the Third World they must often battle with governments to get their ideas of small-scale, decentralist, locally appropriate technologies accepted. Too many of these governments and their friends in industry identify more closely with their counterparts in the affluent nations than with their own people – especially the forgotten ones who live in remote places.

Methane: Fuel of Tomorrow

For longer than history has recorded, men have been fascinated by the 'Will o' the Wisp' – the eerie blue flame which darts over the surface of natural swamps. Now this elusive flame is seen by many survivalists as the 'fuel of the future', a natural gas which can be made from manure and crop residues to cook, heat, light, and even run engines. Almost overnight, centuries of disinterest have been replaced by excited experiment in one country after another, and – as with other alternative energy sources – the experimenters range from small farmers to large organisations such as city sewage authorities. One survivalist I met on my travels was no latecomer.

On the west coast of the United States, between Los Angeles and San Francisco, lies the prosperous town of Santa Barbara. Just a few blocks from its central business district, engulfed by suburbs, is El Mirasol Farm, a four-and-a-half-acre oasis, where volunteers have transformed stiff clay and rubble into an educational and research centre for self-sufficiency based on polyculture – which is the opposite of monoculture. The result is a riot of vegetables, herbs, flowers, grapes, bees and chickens.

The coastal fog had rolled away the day I went to El Mirasol, and the Californian sun burned hot. In the heart of the farm I found an Englishman tending a flame. He wore a look of intense concern. The flame mattered deeply to him, that much was plain, and as I listened to him, I learned the link between that flame, flickering in the midday heat, and the past 20 years of John Fry's life.

John Fry left the Royal Air Force after the Second World War and emigrated to South Africa, where he built up a pig farm from scratch. It took him five years of hard work to make the farm look like paying, but even then one formidable obstacle stood in the way: two tons of wet pig manure a day! He tried composting it, but was beaten by the enormous amount of work . . . carting, heaping, spreading, digging under. He would look at the growing mountain despairingly: there must be *some* use for it; the problem was to find one. It was then that he heard of experiments to make methane gas from chicken droppings, and he decided to see if the idea would work with pig manure.

He learned that highly volatile methane gas was a source of heat and light or could be used to run engines. He learned that it was the result of a bacterial process called anaerobic decay, which occurs in nature, and can be mimicked by putting organic material into airtight containers, where the naturally occurring bacteria multiply and digest the material. When this happens, methane gas builds up as a by-product, which simply has to be led off and stored until needed.

He experimented with a couple of ordinary oil drums and found that the process worked, and from then on John Fry became a man inspired. To the horrified amazement of his friends, he sunk all his money into a digester big enough to supply power for all the farm's heavy work. He knew nothing of engineering and the only construction work he had ever undertaken was building pigsties. But by the end of 1957, the digester was producing gas, and he was ready to start on an engine room. From a scrapyard he bought a rust-covered 13-horsepower diesel power plant, cleaned it, installed it, fitted it with spark-plugs and a mass of gadgetry and connected it to the digester. The contraption not only worked, · it ran night and day for six years. Each day 26 barrowloads of manure were tipped into a shallow container, mixed with some

200 gallons of water and pumped by electricity into the digester, out of which came not only gas but effluent, and excellent fertiliser he could pump on to the land. Gone were the stench, dust, flies and hard work. And the farm had ample power. John Fry reckoned that the gas alone paid for the whole installation within three or four years, but he was saved a greater sum in labour costs and more again in the value of the fertiliser.

In time his neighbours ate their words, and the farm became a showplace, drawing hundreds of visitors a year. Methane had got into his blood and he couldn't settle down. He knew he had stumbled on something significant, and he wanted to demonstrate it. After a fruitless trip to the US and abortive attempts to interest the United Nations, he decided to sell out and return with his family to England. 'I spent five months building and operating a methane composter on a pig farm in England, and it worked just as it was supposed to,' he explained. 'But the people running the farm decided they didn't want to produce and use the gas after all. That left us sort of stranded, so we moved to the United States and in 1965 we finally settled in Santa Barbara.'

Repeated disappointments had exacted a toll, however, and from then on John Fry was plagued with heart trouble. It was not until he was 'discovered' by local environmental organisations that he was able to get back to worthwhile experimenting, culminating in El Mirasol. There, helped by ecologist Richard Merrill, of Santa Barbara, and the New Alchemy Institute, he has designed and set up test plants of various sizes, using a variety of materials. One of his contributions to methane generation has been a digestion unit of horizontal design. Most units were vertical; they clogged up and had to be put out of action for cleaning out and for adding fresh batches of material. John Fry called his design a 'displacement digester' because the material is pushed steadily through a long, flat tank as more is added from a filler pipe at one end.

Another contribution – and this may turn out to be of greater significance – is a very small unit made from scrap, designed for tropical countries of the Third World. John Fry demonstrated it when I went to see him. 'It's a small unit made from scrap inner tubes,' he explained. 'You take a truck-size inner tube, cut right across it and draw the two ends over this plastic insert – the heart of the system, and the only part that has to be specially made. Using an old bicycle inner tube you attach an inlet bucket and pour in a shovelful of manure a day. Once the bacteria have got to work, the gas comes out of another part of the plastic insert, and can be led via some more scrap tubes to an old oil drum, inverted over water, to store it. You get about five cubic feet of gas a day from it – enough to cook one simple meal or bring half a gallon of water to the boil and keep it there for 20 minutes. The idea is that it should be used for poor people in tropical countries who most of the time have nothing to cook with but a little bit of dried dung. The usual practice is to burn it, but then there is nothing to return to the soil; also the smoke is so bad for the eyes that it causes blindness. It was VITA who inspired this equipment. They asked me to do something with materials that any Asiatic person could find in quantity, and this is my answer. Only the plastic insert needs to be made, and that could be moulded cheaply by the million – if only someone were interested.'

John Fry has other ideas too: kelp, cactus, weeds as source material; the throwaway parts of crops such as sisal . . . fish guts from processing factories; he even visualises 'gas farms' growing crops specially for fuel. But his paramount interest is the vast, overall potential of anaerobic digestion, 'the only natural process that hasn't yet been exploited'. He makes his point emphatically: 'Instead of admitting that life is a cycle in which decomposed life is a prerequisite for new life, we've forgotten that the bottom half of the circle doesn't exist. But it *does*, and what excites me is to explore this half and use it to build new life and energy.'

Another survivalist who has pioneered work with methane is Ram Bux Singh, who for 18 years has directed experiments at the Gobar Gas Research Station at Ajitmal in northern India. There he has made simple methane plants small enough to run economically in farms and villages. Since the 'energy crisis', news of his work has spread far beyond his own district, and his straightforward approach has great significance for the future, not only for the Third World, but also for the 'effluent' societies, whose insatiable appetite for energy is measurable by their mountainous excretions of usable waste.

During a recent visit to the USA he told how he had designed units for as little as $100. A farmer or a group of people could now make their own self-contained system to recycle plant and animal waste into high-quality fertiliser and produce a non-polluting fuel for cooking, heating, and running farm machinery. 'A bio-gas plant,' he said, 'can make a farm more self contained and independent.' Or, as his interviewer put it: 'While the radicals *talk* about it, you're *really* bringing power to the people!'

Ram Bux Singh believes that, as the costs of energy and chemical fertilisers rise together, and as population growths demand more intensive agriculture, farmers in developed nations will have to revert to natural nutrients for their crops, and think more and more about methane as a source of both power and high-quality fertiliser. He has found by laboratory tests that when fertiliser is made from methane digesters no nutrients are lost: it is three times richer in nitrogen than ordinary compost.

The Gobar – 'gobar' is Hindi for 'cow dung' – Gas Research Station has not confined its research to rural problems. In several cities it has built plants to process sewage, and, although their main aim has been to clean up the city environment, with skilled supervision the by-products can be put to good use. In Delhi, at the biggest of such plants, the methane drives four 400-horse-power engines for generating electricity – and nearby farmers get the fertiliser free.

Ram Bux Singh is highly critical of the way Western societies ignore the potential energy of their prolific waste – Britain alone throws away some 20 million tons of rubbish a year. He quotes garbage, vegetable trimmings, spoiled food and leftover, human and animal excreta . . . even grass clippings and weeds. All this he sees as input for methane digesters, large and small. For him, even waste bath water has a use: since digesters work best at temperatures over 75 degrees Fahrenheit, this waste hot water could be used to heat suitable insulated family-size digesters, and in this way help solve a temperature problem which a hot country such as India escapes.

Like other non-polluting alternative energy sources, methane is remarkably versatile, but, although it has gained publicity as an alternative to petrol for running cars, this is its least likely application; for unless the gas is compressed – an operation prohibitively high in energy cost – the low-pressure methane fuel containers weigh ten times the ordinary petrol tank! Wherever storage is no problem methane *will* power engines to generate electricity or drive machinery, just as it will provide direct energy to cook and heat and light. In a new, saner society, methane may well live up to the prophecy of survivalists who have worked with it: the fuel of the future.

Muscle Power

To the sun, the wind, water, and methane one other non-polluting alternative source of energy must be added: muscle power! In the scramble to grow food for humans on every available acre, we have replaced animal power with tractor power, on the dubious assumption that there will always be oil to feed them.

Human power too is on the decline, because, as Professor J. K. Galbraith so succinctly put it, the high standard of living to which the world aspires is simply an arrangement for avoiding muscular exertion, and increasing sensual pleasure and over-eating.

Members of the imposed society have become conditioned to ride to work, where machines do the exertion, ride home, flick switches to cook and heat . . . and then work up a sweat by hitting or chasing a ball, or by pedalling a stationary 'bike', rowing a fixed 'boat' or pitting their strength against contraptions of springs and weights . . . all classic examples of needs perverted to wants! They miss the joyful experience of mind, hands, and body united in satisfying work, and their mental and physical health suffers.

Luckily a remedy is at hand, and some survivalists have been quick to leap – if not on the bandwagon – on the humble bike. Philip Brachi, of BRAD at Eithin y Gaer, is a keen alternative technologist with a burning faith in this neglected personal transport mode. Along with many others who live in the country, he has found that, although the car has ousted the local bus service, the bicycle rides supreme. He describes it as: 'A source of pleasure and mobility perfectly suited to the human scale, neither endangering others nor bruising their freedoms; comprehensible, and with a transparent honesty of form and operation; ecologically meek; such a device should need no defence.' He has found the total 'energy cost' of mining and manufacturing one bicycle to be equal to about 250 kilowatt hours or a mere seven gallons of petrol. As for riding it, with 40,000 food calories equalling a gallon of petrol, any non-athletic cyclist can expect to do the equivalent of a cool 1,500 miles per gallon!

Alternative technology is far from perfect: considering its newness, its lack of funding and the lack of experience among its proponents, it would be astonishing if it were! It is vulnerable to criticism, especially in its efforts to harness what appear to be the free energy sources of sun, wind, water, and methane. For as some members of the Technical Research Division of the Cambridge Department of Architecture stated in 1973, alternative technology, at least in its present stage of development, appears to be a more expensive way of doing things than its conventional counterparts. Unless you are careful, small-scale projects, for example, can achieve the opposite of their stated objectives and use up *more* finite resources rather than less, especially if they are duplicated enough times to represent real solutions for society's problems, rather than one-man ego trips. The critics found, moreover, that the smaller the scale you adopt, the more the costs can rise. But if alternative technology is suspect, so too are the economics and accounting methods used to evaluate it, focusing as they do on the narrow goal of 'efficiency' without producing an ethically satisfying answer to the question of 'efficiency for what?' For instance, by concentrating on only *part* of industrial output – the desired product – and ignoring the undesired output of waste and pollution in their costings so that their costs are borne by the community and the biosphere, conventional economies are anything but a reliable yardstick.

Peter Harper is not content to let it rest there, however. In a shrewd assessment, he writes: 'Apparent successes of cheap AT have on the whole been through hidden subsidies of time or resources which could not be generalised throughout society. At the moment, only those with very unusual tastes (such as Spartan living), or those who place an extremely high value on environmental purity, or those who think that the relative positions of "straight" and "alternative" economics will change remarkably, would find it rational to pay the full cost of ATs.'

Certainly alternative technology has shortcomings and many survivalists are guilty of making extravagant claims. Nevertheless, if there is any sense in what they stand for, and if we are to consider the needs of man and the planet, a radically different approach to the generation and use of energy is inescapable. At the risk of committing the sin of 'blueprintism' I would summarise the survivalists' views along the following lines:

We should conserve coal, gas, and oil reserves as long as possible, and in mining them we should not put life at risk – neither human life nor life in the biosphere at large. We should save oil for work which only oil can do: essentially for mobile power units such as farm tractors and for vital transport. Squandering oil on personal private transport, on mass tourism and exotic projects such as Concorde becomes inadmissible. Oil not required for food production and vital transport should be saved for making *lasting* things which fulfil genuine human needs; it should be used either as fuel for essential industry, as the raw material for making useful energy-saving products such as building insulation material, or for the valuable chemicals it contains.

In industry, agriculture, commerce, transport, and the provision of other services, our accounting methods should not be based exclusively on money and outmoded concepts of capital, but on a system of economics which takes account of energy used and energy wasted, remembering that energy is the one resource which cannot be recycled.

We should examine our lifestyles in terms of the energy they consume, especially what they waste. The implications of such an examination are unlimited, ranging as they do from the purely practical, such as recycling every possible material and insulating buildings to prevent heat loss, to decentralisation in order to save unnecessary transport and travel – even to living communally.

We should switch our resources of brains and money to developing small, non-polluting, decentralised energy sources which make use of renewable resources – chiefly the sun, wind, water, and methane. Wood, which is an indirect form of solar energy, may also be used, though not at a rate faster than it can be grown (not in place of food), nor at the expense of other more durable uses to which it might better be put. As fossil fuel reserves dwindle and energy costs rise, we can expect a rash of interest in macro plans to develop alternative energy sources, such as the damming of whole tidal basins; holes bored deep into the earth's interior to release geothermal energy; huge satellites to collect solar energy and focus it on to earth. These plans have an attractive glamour, but most will be found unacceptable when they are assessed in terms of the *needs* of man and the biosphere. Most of them will be seen simply as means to concentrate even more power in the hands of the already rich and powerful at the expense of the poor – and, moreover, too costly in precious fossil fuel ever to justify them.

We should shut down all existing nuclear power stations, stop work on constructing new ones, and concentrate any available research funds into the continuing problems of coping with radioactive waste and thermal pollution. This implies a recognition that fusion reaction as an alternative to fission, currently in use, is not yet possible nor likely to be 'clean'; it would be fallacious to pin any hopes on it as a salvation which will conveniently arrive before fossil fuel supplies falter.

Instead of channelling research efforts into looking for new, large-scale energy sources and expanding industrial output, we should learn more about the capacity of the biosphere to accept even the current levels of pollution. If they are found to be too high, we shall have to reduce supply and demand; if it can accept more, we should learn what is the threshold. Having done so, it is a relatively easy matter to calculate how much energy each person on earth is entitled to use. This done, it will become evident that any nation – or individual – using more than this figure is endangering the survival of others, and we can work towards achieving a more equable distribution of energy throughout the world.

The present energy consumption per head in Western-style nations is an impossible goal for all the people of the world: the resources are simply not there, any more than the capital to exploit them; moreover even if they were, we should all speedily perish in the ensuing thermal pollution. Only one solution remains: to 'de-develop' the rich nations and to halt the spread of 'Western' consumer-oriented ideologies to the Third World. This means adopting a whole new set of values. It means discarding the belief that happiness can be found by trying to satisfy ever-escalating wants, and substituting one which recognises that all people have a right to their basic needs, both material and spiritual – the needs which are least in conflict with the needs of the biosphere.

Such a disparate group of people as the survivalists are clearly not in accord with all of this rudimentary survival plan: for every question it attempts to answer, it begs a thousand more! But on one point there is general agreement: the need for a new set of values. And each survivalist, in his own way, is searching for a clearer definition of it and the means to bring it into being.

Chapter Four:
Somewhere to live

Deep in the Buckinghamshire countryside lies a village which stands on a belt of witchert, a kind of clay, found only in a small area. Witchert is no ordinary clay. It is a superb building material. It lasts: cottages in the village built hundreds of years ago still stand, firm and dry. It keeps out the summer heat and holds in the warmth from winter fires. It is easy to use, and it is cheap – you dig it up from where you want to build. For years the village was a place for villagers: no houses fell down, few were added and, when they were, witchert was used without question. The village enjoyed great character, beauty, and harmony. Then quite suddenly the commuters from progressive Aylesbury discovered it. First they bought up all the available cottages, and after that the speculators moved in smartly with 'executive homes'.

One winter's day, when building is in full swing, a lone survivalist, visiting a friend in the village, strolls up to the site. He sees that lorries, loaders, dumpers and 'dozers have churned up the ground until it is a quagmire; he learns that work is behind schedule and that the men, brought in from the city, are unanimous about the culprit – 'this bloody clay'. A lorry arrives and the survivalist watches them slipping about as they unload the bricks it has brought. He reads the print on the bricks' polythene wrapping. It says 'Made in Belgium'.

Just possibly the new people destined to live in the village would have preferred houses built like the old ones – enjoying some sort of connection with the village. But that was a question no one asked, and, if someone had, doubtless good reasons would have been given as to why the idea was preposterous.

There is nothing very surprising about all this. The building industry, which exists to fulfil one of man's most basic needs, is firmly in the hands of bureaucrats, financiers and other 'experts', far removed from people and the environment.

Whether building for the affluent or underprivileged, they foster the apathy which conditions people to the homes they are offered. As Sim van der Ryn observed, it is a kind of persecution: they can no longer participate in building their own homes; they accept the built-in values of the imposed society, and a spiralling descent into unquestioning helplessness.

But this is not all. In a time of self-inflicted energy crisis, while the most visible offenders, such as the car and aircraft industries, come in for voluble criticism, the building industry gets off almost scot-free. Planners, architects, builders and even home-buyers themselves are all offenders in condoning an endless, unpublicised energy spree of grotesque proportions. For while the industry is hedged in by every kind of restriction designed to perpetuate the mysticism of its professionals, it pays scant regard to the unnecessary energy used in mining and making its materials, in the distances they are transported, and in building methods employed.

Even this irresponsibility, however, is eclipsed by the way architects and bureaucrats have allowed thermal energy to fritter away in the homes they have designed. Nearly half the coal, gas, and electricity used in Britain goes in heating, cooking, lighting, and otherwise powering homes. Heating accounts for most of it, yet reliable estimates show that in an average non-insulated house roughly 75 per cent of the energy used in heating is lost through walls, windows, and roof; in contrast, an insulated house *retains* roughly 73 per cent. According to J. J. Burke, managing director of ICI insulation service, it is technically and economically possible to halve the maximum thermal energy demand for housing in Britain. And a report, prepared jointly by Friends of the Earth and Age Concern, states that if adequate insulation standards were enforced nationally they could avoid the need for 50 nuclear reactors costing some £10,000 million!

Waste is not confined to energy. As the writer, Terence McLaughlin, has observed: 'We transport water miles from the water works, make it slightly dirty (at the rate of 30 gallons a day per person) and then send it miles to the sewage works to be purified . . . We pipe our sewage away, sometimes into the sea, and then buy artificial fertilisers that themselves use up energy in their production.' He might also have added that poisonous nitrates from excessive use of fertilisers then leach into underground water supplies, and for this little problem the technocrats' predictable answer is to build high-technology purifiers – which use still more energy!

Materials, sewage, and energy are not the only finite resources squandered. Housing, along with industry and commerce, sprawls shamefully over land desperately needed for food and recreation. The critical problem of designing humane high-density living remains unanswered, and the long-favoured solution of high-rise towers has been shown to generate intolerable social tensions. In one survey, 86 per cent of high-rise dwellers said they would rather live in a house in a street. But even there, the typical suburban home fails to offer a satisfactory environment: it perpetuates the restrictive nuclear family and alienates the inhabitant from his surroundings.

In short, the building industry pays scant attention to satisfying people's basic needs and, by squandering energy and finite resources, it shows little regard for the needs of the biosphere. Despite great odds, the whole subject of shelter is one where the survivalists have been most active. It was one of the most exciting aspects of my journey.

Grass Root Research

The busy main road between Ely and Chatteris runs unswervingly through the bleak, flat fen country of Cambridgeshire – a route for container juggernauts shuttling to and from East Coast ports, and for lorries heaped with sugar beet from the black, peaty soil of the district's immense farms. The traffic thunders a mere ten feet from 'The Horse and Gate', where, in more leisurely days, a narrower road was kinder to the Victorian house, and travellers stopped to slake their thirst.

It is no longer a pub, and time is too precious for today's travellers even to slow down; as the house flashes past them, they could hardly know that on this unlikely site two university graduates, Brenda and Robert Vale, have sunk their slender savings into experiments in survival.

When an architectural student has spent the statutory five years' hard labour of learning he usually bends over backwards to get a job which will pay dividends rich enough to reward him for the deprivation. Brenda and Robert Vale chose otherwise. When they finished at Cambridge University they chose to buy 'The Horse and Gate' and its two acres where they could do work that no government department, university, or company seemed to have time for.

At the University they had been attached to the Technical Research Division which had been studying academically the technology and economics of autonomous housing – dwellings independent of outside services for heating, lighting, water, and drainage. Both husband and wife had written on the subject; each had designed sophisticated examples of the challenging concept, but they felt frustrated. As Brenda put it: 'I built this fantastic model . . . but that's about as far as one gets with any of these projects.' In short, research seemed to have become an end in itself: more than anything else, they wanted to get out and do something!*

'If autonomous servicing or alternative technology is to have any point,' Robert Vale declares, 'you've got to adapt it to a *new* autonomous house – we know that; but how many people are prepared to knock down all the old houses and replace them with new ones – or can afford to? So it's got to be sort of "clipped on" to old houses, and what we're trying to do is demonstrate this.' But the goal of autonomy doesn't stop at the walls of the house. As survivalists they are also interested in achieving as near

---

*The Vales have written a book of practical solutions. *The Autonomous House: Design and Planning for Self-Sufficiency* (Universe Books, 1975).

self-sufficiency in food as possible. 'We're trying to develop these two acres to produce as much as possible for us and our animals – to cultivate very intensively, but not chemically. And the only way is to *try* it – there's nothing in books about anything as small as two-acre holdings.'

The £12,000 property was all they could afford, a compromise, and even *that* took some finding. 'I'd prefer to live somewhere that wasn't on a main road,' Robert admits, 'somewhere that's rather hard to get to; an idyllic place would be nice to live in, but this one is more realistic. Most people can't get an idyllic place because they usually go at high prices as second homes for city people. And most people have to manage on much less land. We couldn't find five acres, and with land at £1,000 an acre we couldn't have afforded more anyway.'

They recognised from the outset that full self-sufficiency was not on, that there would always be the need for an income, and this influenced the choice of site. During the setting-up period, Robert has worked full-time for an architect in Cambridge, and Brenda two days a week in an Ely bookshop, but they soon found that this left too little time to work in the house and on the land. 'I work much more than I want to,' he complains. 'I'd like to have a part-time job, but where I work it has to be full-time or not at all.'

Their aim has been to reduce the dependence of the house on inputs from the system, and this is fully possible in summer, but only partly in winter. The key lies in concentrating on insulation, solar heating, wind-generated electricity, and methane gas production. 'I don't think an old house can ever be fully autonomous,' Robert contends. 'They're not the right shape, the roofs aren't optimised for solar collection and there isn't room to put in vast insulated storage tanks for water, you need to store summer heat through the winter – not without completely rebuilding.'

In their first winter of 1973–74, they installed an imported Finnish wood-burning stove and used an existing anthracite burning stove for cooking and water heating . . . 'and we were very cold!' Robert recalls. If anything needed to, this experience pushed insulation high up their list of priorities: 'We're insulating the house with two inches of glass fibre and half an inch of expanded polyurethene in the walls, and four to five inches of glass fibre in the roof. These aren't "soft" materials in environmental resource impact level: ideally we should be using straw and old newspapers and egg boxes and things, which could be someone's argument. But on the other hand, we argue that one might as well make the world's remaining oil into nice insulating boards which will last forever rather than burn it up in central heating.

'We thought of doing it from the outside, because that would have been elegant, and we could have made the finished house much bigger, but you run into all sorts of dreadful problems about the window sills, and what you cover the insulation with to stop water getting in. That was going to be expensive, we decided, so we're doing it on the inside and it's all a compromise between insulation and not losing 20 square feet off the house because we've brought the walls in a foot. So we're having about two-and-a-half inches of insulation covered with plaster board, and this means we can heat the whole three-bedroom house with about three kilowatts.

'We've got to burn *some* sort of fuel because we can't get enough heating from the sun and wind. I suppose we could have a very big windmill, but we can't afford to buy one and we haven't the skills or workshop to build one. We've got to burn something and we've got to burn it in the house where it will be about 400 per cent more efficient than heating by mains electricity. We thought originally we'd burn wood, because that would be very nice, and it *grows*, and people don't have to go down and dig it up, and it's all . . . "softer". But there aren't a lot of woods around us in the Fens, and we'd have to import the wood, so we ended up by deciding on a coal-burning stove which will cook and heat water – the coalman lives next door, which is some factor! And if we put it in the centre of a very highly insulated house, all the heat from it will stay in. We'll also have the log stove for emergencies and for burning rubbish on, and this will give roughly three kilowatts.'

In summer they expect to get plenty of hot water from 15 square metres of solar collector mounted on the roof. This is made of corrugated aluminium, painted black, over which flows the water to be solar-heated. To intensify the heat, the aluminium is covered with corrugated polyvinyl, fluoride-coated glass fibre, and then with glass. To be environmentally pure they would prefer to use all glass for the covering, because it is made of common materials and can be melted down, but glass has to be supported in glazing bars, whereas corrugated plastic does not.

Autonomous lighting has presented no problem, as Robert explains: 'We've got two Lucas "Freelite" wind generators which we saw in *Exchange and Mart*, going very cheap £25 each – because nobody wants them now that they're all "on the electric". These are going on telegraph poles – the planning people seem very happy we should put them up. Apparently we have a progressive planning officer. Each windmill generates 200 watts – 12 volts – which will give a kilowatt hour a day . . . enough to run all our lighting, gramophone, wireless . . . you know, all the good things of life, provided we use fluorescent tubes, which I don't like very much, but are much more efficient. So we've got to wire up the house separately with a 12-volt power system. A 12-volt fluorescent light only takes 13 watts which gives the equivalent of a 75-watt light bulb. We hope one windmill will be enough to provide all our electricity and we won't need any other source eventually.'

The Vales share the sense of outrage felt by all survivalists that so much effort and technology, so many resources, are diverted prudishly to flushing the nation's fertility-rich sewage into the long-suffering sea. They had hoped to opt out of the scandal, but soon found that Health Authorities will not allow any sewage system other than the conventional mains drainage or at best a septic tank, because, as Robert puts it: 'They don't like you to do anything with your own sewage.' However, they hope to overcome this obstacle: 'The Authorities can't force you to *use* the mains drainage,' he points out. 'It sounds a bit fascist, I know, but we might have to sell the house one day and we might not be lucky enough to sell it to some happy "eco-freak" who wants to go out to a little shed in the garden. So we don't actually envisage pouring concrete down the bog on the great day we stop using the mains services, and we'll keep the mains connected – just in case. Mind you, there's nothing to stop you building a methane digester and connecting a bog to it, and having a shed in the garden to which you retire occasionally – I mean, you don't have to *tell* anybody. But it isn't fantastically worth it because your own contribution to the overall gas production isn't worth anything . . . at least, not worth going out into the cold for.'

At the time we talk, the food production side of the enterprise consists of vegetables, some hens, two goats and half a Jersey cow. 'We thought we'd start off with goats,' Robert explains, 'because they're smaller, and they only have two teats and you've only got two hands, and you haven't got to swap around all the time, doing one end and then the other. The thing about goat's milk is that it makes lovely yoghurt, but when you start making it into cheese it *looks* nice – like Gruyère, with great holes in it – but it doesn't *taste* nice, because there's more short-chain fatty acids in it which give it a "goaty" taste. Brenda eats it because she has better willpower, and the hens like it.

'It was a nice stage in the self-sufficiency process when we told the milkman he wasn't to come any more. Either we had to accept this problem as a fact of goat life, or else keep a cow. So we bought a Jersey cow which we share with the chap who runs the bookshop where Brenda works, and we now make butter, very good hard cheese, and cream. We're going to keep the goats as well because they eat different things from cows and they'll give milk when the cow is dry and vice-versa.'

You don't have to be long with this quiet, shy young couple to sense not only how much they enjoy what they are doing, but how much, for all their gaiety and Robert's dry humour, they burn with deep conviction to see it through. The ever-present problem is the shortage of money and time. 'We get up at ten to seven,' Brenda tells me, 'Robert goes to work first, I feed the animals and, on the days I work, I catch the 8.30 bus. I get home about six, he gets home at quarter-to-seven, so we eat and then do the goats and cow and shut the animals up and then start other jobs. Everybody says "How on earth do you manage?" but when it comes to it . . . you just manage. I find the more you take on, the more time and energy you seem to have.'

They are hoping to persuade someone else nearby to co-operate on a similar venture, and as a first step they already share the cow and machinery with a neighbour. Robert is acutely conscious of the time and money constraints: 'If you come from peasant stock, and had lived on some farm for ages and ages, there'd be a great multitude of little structures you could keep hens, geese or pigs in, but if you haven't you've got to build them first out of this and that.

'You keep getting distracted. We were just starting the job of insulating the house when the one existing farm building we had – the hen house – started to disintegrate. It hadn't been looked after, and it had woodworm and dry rot and things, and it began to fall apart and there were hens sort of falling out of it. So we had to stop what we were doing and build a new one, and that took a long time because we could only work in the evenings. The trouble is, I'm probably not a very good smallholder, because I like to build beautiful structures which will last a hundred years and then we won't have to re-build them when we're old. And this takes time . . .'

I ask Robert how close to self-sufficiency he thinks they can become. 'We can get enough vegetables off three-quarters of an acre,' he says. 'It depends a lot on how much of a vegetarian you are. I'm not sure I'd like to be entirely vegetarian. We're not vegetarians and we eat the odd hens. Hens eat an awful lot – you'd be surprised how much.

'The prospects for vegetable-growing are excellent, the seeds are so cheap. You sow a packet of marrow seeds and you get about 400 lbs of marrows! It's very gratifying. You don't cost your labour because what else would you be doing if you weren't digging the garden, which you like doing anyhow? This is the theory. But basically, what we're doing – to be self-sufficient – nobody wants to do at all . . . apart from the middle classes, because it happens to be in the *Sunday Times* at the moment. That passes. To actually grub about in the ground and kill hens and eat them and all the rest of it doesn't appeal.' Then he asks the crucial question: 'How do you do all this, given a system which doesn't want to do it? It's hard to get out of it.'

Brenda and Robert, who have taken the first steps, quietly get on with insulating their house and tending their two acres. They have taken steps to satisfy most of the basic human needs: food, shelter, and warmth, a sense of belonging, control over their lives, creative work in a situation which lies within their ability to cope, together with the stimulation of constant fresh challenges – all with minimal harm to the biosphere. And ten feet away the container juggernauts and the sugar beet lorries thunder by remorselessly, just in case they should ever forget how close to them the system remains.

The problem which the Vales are tackling dominates others: the conversion of existing houses and flats to reduce their energy appetite. Imperfect though these dwellings are, they do exist, and to pull them down to build perfect structures would be sheer lunacy.

In an energy-hungry world an unpalatable truth faces overdeveloped countries such as Britain and the USA. These countries face short-term population increases, but in relative terms the increases are small. Despite what the growth pundits say, the extra people to come could be accommodated in *existing* housing stock, supplemented by only a modest programme of new building. In affluent societies many people own two homes; many live in homes far bigger than they need; and in large tracts of country empty houses are decaying. A sample census in Britain during 1966 showed that, while overcrowding was rife, over a million single people were living in five rooms or more – and the picture is unlikely to be any brighter today. A survey subsequently conducted for the Greater London Housing Committee showed that in London alone there would be 136,000 rooms to spare for people on the housing waiting list if over-housed tenants could be persuaded to move to something smaller. Nearly 100,000 homes had more rooms than the families living in them needed; often as well, older couples lived on alone in houses far too large for them once their children had left home. The inescapable truth is that over-large houses could be shared or divided into flats; that, with a policy of decentralisation, rural areas could be revitalised and crumbling houses saved; moreover, with the emergence of a new set of social values, many people could live communally, more happily than they do now, consuming less energy and resources – as survivalists have found the world over. With such a U-turn in society, the only major building effort would be a twofold programme, much kinder to the planet: to convert existing homes; and to build new homes for people moving from cities, which have no future, into a countryside crying out for new life.

Establishment Research
One notable attempt at converting existing homes has been the work of a team led by Steven Szokolay, who in 1974 left the Polytechnic of Central London to take up a post in Australia. Before he left he explained to me that his team had been aiming at the largest mass-market: Local Authority housing for people who expect to bath whenever they want to – not just when the sun is shining. With a rare grant from the Department of the Environment the team was able to design a solar heating system that could be literally bolted into a standard house – and save no less than 63 per cent of its annual heating fuel requirements!

At the time, a large housing estate was under construction at the New Town of Milton Keynes, and the team was able to install its equipment in one of the estate's standard houses – '. . . a thermally rather inefficient building, with insulation just satisfying the regulations . . .,' as Steven Szokolay described it. A critical decision was the size of the solar collector area, and members of the team worked out that under average chilly January radiation conditions, collector plates covering 40 square metres – about half the size of the floor area – would provide just enough heat. To store this heat they chose water as the medium, and worked out that an insulated tank of just over five cubic metres would hold a day's heat requirements in the crucial mid-winter. Dull periods had to be allowed for, and so, as an auxiliary supply to keep the water up to the necessary 104°F, they added an electric immersion heater; to disseminate the heat they installed a fan-convector unit. For winter conditions the domestic hot water system also needed an auxiliary heater to maintain a desired 140°F, a temperature attainable in summer directly from the collectors.

Calculations showed that, for the installation to be justified by the fuel saved over a 10-year period, its capital cost should be no more than £665. In practice it turned out to be three times this amount, but Steven Szokolay stressed two important factors: firstly, it was a 'hand-tooled job made for at least twice the *realistic* manufactured cost; secondly, fuel costs, prevailing at the time the sums were done, were rising steeply. When these factors were taken into account, the installation's viability seemed no longer in doubt, he maintained.

The Milton Keynes house was a compromise to meet a realistic situation, but it is the dream of most eco-architects to design and build a *fully* autonomous house: one which needs no power input at all, whether from coal, gas or oil; which has no water supply other than rain, and no sewers to carry away waste.

In the Department of Architecture at Cambridge University, two alternative designs are evolving, one by Alexander Pike, the department's director, and the other by James Thring and Gerry Smith, two of his research assistants. Both designs draw on three years of research, which has been financed chiefly by a rare grant from the Science Research Council, and backed by help in construction from the Department of the Environment and some manufacturing organisations.

This work has shown that the autonomous house, while not the answer to city and suburban problems, can come into its own in places where population densities are low, for there the costs of providing central services of power, sewage and refuse collection are out of proportion. For example, when density falls from forty people to the acre to four people, they jump by 300 per cent. This means that in rural districts extra costs in building a high technology autonomous house can be offset by savings in power lines, gas and sewerage pipes and in refuse collection.

The two Cambridge designs have strong similarities: they both involve recycling the household water; both use solar energy for space heating, and store the heat of summer in huge underground insulated water tanks for gradual release throughout the winter months; both envisage using wind power and also methane digesters for cooking, the gas being generated from the unit's animal, vegetable and human wastes. The designs differ mainly in their shape: the Pike house is rectangular, the other octagonal; there are also differences in the way that various components have been integrated and problems solved.

Alexander Pike, who prefers 'autarchic' to autonomous, states that such a house could become the centre of a wholly self-supporting unit for a family of four if it were set in one and three-quarters of an acre, carrying a couple of goats and a dozen hens for protein needs, along with intensive vegetable production.

Robert and Brenda Vale, who were originally members of the team, have each designed an autonomous house using similar principles. The Eithin y Gaer community chose Robert's design for its second house on the other side of the hill; and Brunel Environment Group picked Brenda's design for the one they hope to build within the campus.

Kit Pedler at his home in Clapham, working alone to achieve similar ends, is highly sceptical of the fully autonomous house concept for a country such as Britain. 'On the basis of presently available technology,' he says, 'even the most enthusiastic of autonomous house designers will have to accept that, in Britain's urban area, sunlight and wind power will not together provide all the energy needed.' He plans to supplement 'natural' energy with power from a small gas engine, chosen because it will run either from the house's methane digester or from the gas mains, as circumstances dictate. Exhaust gases from the engine will be cooled by a heat exchanger, their heat being fed into the house's central energy store – a highly insulated, high-capacity water tank. This will be filled from filtered rainwater which will be used over and over again – a design factor that rules out detergents in favour of soap. Anyone repelled by the idea of using recycled water may take heart from knowing that in the south of England most mains water has already been used at least once. If you *must* drink bathwater, your own probably has an aesthetic edge over other people's!

Albuquerque Episode

On my journey into the alternative I set out to find, wherever I could, those survivalists who were working seriously on novel designs with both new and indigenous materials. 'Go west,' people said, 'go to New Mexico: there you will find exciting people mindful of new "ecologically benign" houses for remote areas.' And so I found myself in Albuquerque, a brash, sprawling, fully-motorised city which, it seemed, had mushroomed almost overnight from the surrounding desert. Amply endowed with sunshine, technocrats, and dollars, Albuquerque had apparently attracted a number of experimenters in survival. I set forth to meet them.

I had previously written to Gene R. Bussey, of Life Support Systems Incorporated, so I promptly telephoned him, reminding him that I had come to see him. He was sorry but he was too busy, he said – and our conversation was over in two minutes flat. A bad start. I telephoned Steve Baer of Zomeworks Corporation: he had received my letter and could see me later that afternoon. Things looked better: meanwhile I telephoned Robert Reines, of Integrated Life Support Systems Laboratories, who were new to me; after a long talk with some kind of press officer and a further call while they 'checked up' I was told that a car would pick me up from Zomeworks, when I was through around 17.30. Things began to look promising.

I already knew something of Steve Baer: that he had been one of the hippies of the sixties who had pioneered the dome cult, that he had helped build Drop City, making domes from the tops of junked motor cars to show how scrap could be turned into cheap housing. I knew that he had progressed from dome to 'Zome' – a geometric shape with a parallel zone in it, more flexible than a dome for its ability to stretch and join on to other Zomes; and that he had built a 'Zome' house for his family, said to get 85 per cent of its heating from the sun, despite the arid region's bitter winter nights. I was aware that this $40,000, 2,000-square-foot house had several unique features. Instead of conventional solar collectors, it had a south wall stacked with 90 ordinary 55-gallon drums filled with water. Ranged behind glass panels, their blackened ends absorbed heat by day and radiated it into the house at night. To prevent heat loss at night, wall-length insulating flaps, hinged at ground level, could be hauled up around sunset to seal the wall, and lowered in the morning. In the roof were 'Skylids' – Steve's patented ventilators – activated by the sun to open and close automatically and so help maintain a constant inside temperature. Finely balanced, they worked without switches or motors, using the expansion properties of heat-sensitive Freon gas in cannisters. The main walls of the house comprised several big sandwiches of two aluminium skins laminated to a cardboard honeycomb core; for maximum insulation, urethene foam was blown into the core of each 'sandwich' from both sides, leaving an inch of dead air space in the centre. Apart from this, I had heard that, although the ex-hippy was now a businessman, he was still deeply concerned about the dangers of excessive power in the hands of scientists, government and large corporations; and that, despite his fascination with Zomes and aluminium, he still believed in low technology adapted to local needs. I had come a long way: I looked forward to meeting the man, his ideas, his house, and his hardware.

While I waited, in a space filled with models, tubing, drawings and magazines, a slightly built, quiet-spoken man passed me a number of times without attracting much attention; after a while he motioned me into a small, bare office. It was not until we had begun talking that I realised this was Steve Baer – less rugged, less relaxed, younger than either his image or his photographs had anticipated. I declared my interest, and by way of an opener I asked how much he thought that the world-wide housing and energy shortage would be helped by a material such as aluminium which took more energy to mine and manufacture than almost any other used for building.

For a second I thought he would vault over the desk. 'Aluminium is a beautiful material,' he rapped out. 'I don't know where it comes from and I don't much care. Why? Because my work here is for America and Americans – I don't want to make houses for Africans or Indians. I like my work – I like aluminium, the way it feels and how it sounds. Okay?'

I said it was some kind of defect I had, but I was more interested in the world than America . . .

'What the world needs,' he said defensively, 'is things that are more simple, more beautiful, that don't keep breaking down, that could have been made by, say, James Watt. A lot of the ideas I've had are ones that could have been made a hundred years ago – and I'm proud of that. I'm all for lateral invention.' He paused in thought. 'Listen . . . a chicken makes chickens, and men make men, but now it's as if a chicken has to stand on a dog and listen to a butterfly. Making things has become too dependent on other things. We need to reverse this trend.'

I asked what he was doing about it at Zomeworks.

'One of the answers is small business; no static. Everyone who works here has a piece of the business – eight or ten people. It's fun to have a business filling a real need. It's an end in itself. Big corporations don't provide it.'

'What kind of people buy what you make?' I asked.

'I sell to the people with money – doctors, lawyers. They buy my Zomes, Skylids, other things, because they're daring. They bring in the money. They'll take a chance with me and my things because they're fed up that everything else is coming out of some big laboratory. I think the whole world is involved in an experiment – in doing something completely different – something crazy...'

'The whole world or America?'

'America anyway. That's why I want to be here: to get those sons of General Motors to think differently. Take a civilisation squandering all its resources and splinter off a group that's going in a different direction ... it *must* be good, even if it's fumbling and making mistakes. It's easy to do better than the establishment when you're aiming at doing things that are rewarding. If the communards like what they're doing – that's fine. Only that kind of energy can start something new. Maybe the planet is evolving a new kind of human species. The world is changing so rapidly today that nobody knows what's going on. Every now and then you'll hear a voice – like Lewis Mumford's – that sounds very clear, but the rest of us are just stumbling around.'

He looked across through the open door of the office and saw someone waiting outside. Baer the prophet switched places with Baer the businessman. He apologised to me, explaining that he had an *important* meeting scheduled – something to do with money – and ushered me out.

Outside his office, among the hardware, I waited for the car that was to take me to my next encounter. I had ample time to make sense of the whirlwind that was my previous one. Like many survivalists, Steve Baer had a vision of a world gone mad. It seemed that his way of surviving in an environment of increasing perplexity was to concentrate his energies onto things American, onto the smaller, familiar world of his materials, his techniques, and his business. I suspected that there he knew what he was doing, whereas outside he saw little hope – only a slim chance that, if the communards and a few innovators like himself continue to do what they *feel* is right, others may take notice. Waiting in the lobby among cross-sections of aluminium and urethene panels, models of Zomes and Skylids, lengths of tubing and wind generator parts, I felt little elation about the prospects for salvation.

Interlude in the Desert

The car that had brought me up into the mountains above Alburquerque swung round sharply, its tyres biting the rough track, as it nosed into a shallow valley. Stark against the bare hillside, three domes gleamed white in the brilliant moonlight. As we pulled in to park I glimpsed wind generators and solar panels. We halted, and a huge dog bounded towards me until checked by a command. I had arrived at the desert site of Integrated Life Support Systems Laboratories, Tijeras, altitude nearly 8,000 feet. A short walk and I had entered the airlock of the nearest dome, Prototype I.

Once through the airlock I found myself in the insulated atmosphere of the dome: soft, shadowless lighting, strange acoustics, unfamiliar shapes, a curious sense of space and detachment from reality. A consol of dials and switches caught my eye: a needle in one dial pointed to 'dome temperature'; in another 'earth temperature'. Before I could see more I was handed a routine security document to sign, guaranteeing that I would write nothing about the laboratories without consent. I had come a long way from Albuquerque and it was a long way back. I signed. I was privileged to be here, for the laboratories were officially closed to visitors.

Before leaving Albuquerque I had been quizzed at length over the phone about my background and motives. From people in that bustling city I had been warned that I would find ILS Laboratories uninformative, because they were sitting on a potential money spinner, about to start producing autonomous housing by mass production. The talk in the car on the way up had been friendly enough, but unrevealing. I was now about to meet the man behind it all.

Robert Reines greeted me warmly and gave me a rapid tour, first of the dome we were in and then the rest of the site. This dome, the prototype, was 31 feet across and 14 feet high, made from steel panels sprayed inside with a three-inch coating of polyurethene foam for insulation and rigidity. At the top was a skylight for light and ventilation; around the sides were portholes. Two-thirds of the ground area was living space, the rest was kitchen, bathroom, toilet, office and storage, over part of which was a sleeping area. Outside, three salvaged, ex-farm, wind generators charged high-capacity storage batteries for lighting, cooking, and appliances. Solar collectors heated 3,000 gallons of water in an insulated storage tank for space heating and for domestic hot water at 150 degrees Fahrenheit. I learned that during the 1972–3 winter they were ten days without sun, and at nights the temperature was sub zero; yet the temperature of the dome was kept at 65 degrees. In summer its temperature could rise to 80 degrees, but a low humidity was said to make this tolerable. By shading the skylight and opening vents at night, the temperature could be reduced to 75 degrees. One of the other domes was a store, the third was the unfinished Prototype II, 20 per cent cheaper to build, and with built-in solar panels and water tank and more window area. The key to the system was its low energy requirements: insulation and absence of cracks reduced heat loss; the spacious white concave interior was adequately lit by a mere 150 watts. I learned that the energy investment in Prototype II equalled that of an average car, and that this energy was close to the difference between the energy consumed by Prototype II and that consumed by a conventional house over a ten-year period. Fifteen people made up the laboratory team, eight living on the site and the rest working whenever they could.

The tour over, we returned to Prototype I and, over coffee heated by the wind, we sat down to talk. Large and shaggy, with a voice to match, Robert Reines reminded me of an amiable bear, and he spoke of ILS with the quiet fervour of a missionary, in the convincing cadences of an orator. 'The space we're sitting in now I designed and built all myself, he began. 'The first space in the world to be totally powered by the sun and the wind. It represents a reasonable investment in energy and materials: once you've dumped the energy into making it, it will run for two hundred years: a piece of hardware that can be built quickly, with great flexibility in design and use of space for the price of a mobile home. People can erect it themselves: it doesn't require experts. It can survive the elements and it has minimal impact on the environment. It requires no back-up from gasoline generators: we have demonstrated that it is technically possible to use the sun and the wind for all our needs – whether they extend to a blender and a refrigerator, or whether they stop at a 40-watt bulb.

'To my mind this is one of the most powerful tools that man has had in centuries, because it allows for individual expression. Because its inner space is flexible, you can change your house; and when you can do that, *you* change too. It gives you a very elegant vehicle in which to step out of society, to look back and decide what you want to take with you and what you want to create yourself, so that you can go off in a new direction.'

From describing his product he switched to the problems of society. People in cities lived too far from the earth, coddled in a self-made air-conditioned womb with limited future; for the industrialised state could no longer guarantee the energy to maintain the womb. He was working to bring about social change by exciting people's imaginations: to show what was possible and what a different world might be like. Yet he was aware of his dependence on society, he maintained: 'Society is where you get the spark plug for your car, and one reason I'm interested in changing society is I need the spark plug! I can't throw society out. I need steel and other materials. We have to save not only ourselves, not only our relatives and friends, not only people who have a common goal structure; we must attempt to save the different societies which exist in the world, and maintain their individuality.

'We have a great responsibility. Here we stand with the hardware that allows people for the first time in history to band together and, with their own economics, build their own energy-autonomous communities on land of low value where there's no sewers, gas, or electricity. This means one thing to the real estate guys – who are not going through any social change – and something else to people who are frustrated and who are really interested in building communities and doing things for themselves. So a lot of the work that we are doing here is concerned with what we should do with this tool and how we can make it a little better in terms of people's needs.

'How do you get it to the people? At present I have no idea. Do you introduce it to society through people who come to you wanting to build communities out of their own efforts for their own ideologies? Or do you put it on the market like the "hula hoop"? But what we would have done with it last year is very different from what we would do with it this year.

'One way to solve some of the society's problems is having people take more from themselves instead of asking for more from others. The people here at ILS Laboratories are hoping never to become rich – just rich in wisdom, experience, and understanding. They work 15 hours a day on essentially no pay; they contribute their time; they put everything on the line – their emotions, their intellects, their concern, their allegiance to make this thing work. We're trying to evolve by taking from ourselves and contributing to a common goal. We're going to make this tool as powerful as we can, but at the same time as humble and receptive and simple as we can.

'There are pressures on the Laboratory from huge corporations that see the economic aspects of what we're doing. A lot of people would like to take what we've got – not many people ever come up with a truly new idea. So one must protect the tool until one has learned how to use it. We have said that ILS will remain a laboratory to develop this and other tools and also to study what happens to people when they live in it and use it. How much space does a person need? More than a closet, less than a castle. What happens when your real needs and your synthetic needs become clear? What is it like to live and work in the same environment? Does the *whole* place become your home, for if so you may only need a very small space for your own territory? What do you do with existing housing stock, faced with an energy crisis? We want the tool to have a certain universality – not just for culture A or B, but for cultures A to Z – which poses some real anthropological and sociological questions. The designer of the tool must be sensitive to the use of the tool. Most designers' attitudes today are related to the corporate form, the growth ethic, minimum lifetime and maximum bucks. The laboratory is now closed so that we may have the freedom to explore some very fundamental questions about people's needs, motivations, and interactions.'

I slept that night in a habitat totally powered by the sun and the wind, and before I left next morning I had learned something of Robert Reines' background and motivation. Having twice dropped out of college he joined the Air Force, armed with a couple of degrees – biology and electrical engineering – and found himself involved in testing nuclear weapons. Two years of this convinced him that he could do something more useful: 'After a point you realise that this kind of work is insane, the mark of a decadent society . . . you're plotting your own death in a round-about way,' was how he put it.

He got himself transferred to a self-created job studying solar energy, and then resigned his commission. He and his wife, Eileen, bought 30 acres of desert and built Prototype I in their spare time with their own hands for $12,000 of their own money. 'When we turned the solar collector on, we were down to our last penny, it was that close,' he confessed.

Long-term he envisaged a community of several hundred people working on new models of living. All he needed was the money and this was the chief problem. As he put it realistically: 'We talk about new life styles, new modes of trying to bring a sense of reason to the social and technological interface so that technology becomes a real slave to human beings. We talk about these things . . . but what do we do about the old buck?'

As I returned to Albuquerque my head buzzed with conflicting impressions. Of the team's total dedication I entertained little doubt – no more than I held for their passionately declared aim of using neglected natural energy. What did bother me was their interpretation of the aim. They had assured me that most of their hardware was 'salvaged' from the system, yet the expenditure per head on energy and finite resources still seemed excessive when related to global availability. I was uneasy about the project's 'space station vibrations' – the sense of total isolation from the natural environment once the dome's airlock had been sealed behind me. I wondered too whether, in their obsession to be self-sufficient in light and heat, the team had lost sight of other dominant inputs – food, fuel for transport, the 'necessities' of American middle-class affluence – which completed the equation. And, above all, however exciting and challenging such experiments might be for the participants, I couldn't help doubting their relevance to the overriding, world-wide problem of reducing mankind's wants and tailoring needs to a biosphere able to support them. And yet, despite all these doubts, I still felt like telling some of the citizens of Albuquerque that they had got Robert Reines wrong. Sure he meant business, but not in the way they meant – the *only* way they were capable of understanding.

Thatch is Beautiful
In the rarified atmosphere of autonomous houses, expanded polystyrene foam insulation, domes and 'zomes', it is easy to forget humble, everyday requirements. Even Steven Szokolay's installation has its limitations, for not every standard house has its roof conveniently facing south, nor has it room for storing large volumes of water – even if the householder can afford the package. Heating the whole house from the sun may be the ideal, but heating just the domestic water is a step not to be scorned – and it can be done simply and cheaply. At reasonable prices a number of companies are now marketing installations which can be mounted on the ground, if your roof happens to be the wrong slope or face the wrong direction. Alternatively, you can do the job yourself.

Spurred on by the 1973 energy crisis and the prospect of soaring fuel costs, John O'Connell in Glamorganshire, with help from a metal worker, built his own installation for £200. Despite unexpected snags, by February 1974 he was able to connect the 24-square-foot collector to his standard 35-gallon hot water tank – and to his delight he found that on sunny days he was heating it to 114°F. On ruling fuel costs he predicted a saving of £50 a year – more as prices rose.

But even home-made solar water heaters involve more than a mite of high technology, and their glamour can detract from the basic world-wide problem of providing any adequate house at all for the countless millions of people throughout the world living in slums, in shanty towns or without *any* kind of home. In the light of *their* problem, a 'Zome' filled with fridge, deep freeze, propane gas stove, laundry machine and other 'necessities' of the affluent society has only marginal relevance. The overwhelming survival requirement of millions is simply a low cost house: described by survivalist Harold Dickinson as 'A house you can't afford, that's cheaper than another house you can't afford'.

Third World workers with first-hand knowledge of Third World problems wryly compare the money and effort spent on research into city-inspired, high-energy technologies and materials with the neglect of natural materials which abound in rural areas. The reasons for this neglect are not hard to find: these materials have no glamour; the techniques they require are labour-intensive; they encourage a developing country to be independent – in short there is no money in them for affluent exporters. Moreover, just as western city dwellers have been conditioned to accept one brand of imposed society, so the more suggestible people of the Third World are becoming conditioned to accept another.

The situation in Botswana in southern Africa is typical. In many parts of the world, the traditional roofing material is thatch, made from grass, reeds, or palm leaves. A well-thatched roof can last up to 15 years; it is lightweight and so exerts small demands on its supporting walls, it is waterproof, and it insulates well from heat and cold. Yet in Botswana thatch has acquired a bad image. It is a sign of the backwardness which the traditional way of life has come to mean. Corrugated iron, cement, and plastic, in contrast – which lack the qualities of thatch – symbolise 'progress'

. . . they are 'modern'. So villagers import them – and become dependent on the cities; the whole nation imports them and becomes dependent on the industrialised West. Poverty is not alleviated – merely modernised.

Beautiful materials and methods such as adobe, rammed earth, clay bricks, pozzolanas, stone, timber, bamboo, wattle, reeds and grass are available throughout the world; and, although some of them have become scarce through neglect or over-cropping, they could be revived. They meet the needs of man; wisely used, they present no conflict with the needs of the biosphere. As with other socially appropriate technologies they call for little energy, for they can be made locally without recourse to high inputs of fossil fuel. Moreover they demand no energy-hungry roads or vehicles to transport them over long distances. These simple materials serve to remind us of the basic problem which affects the building industry no less than any other industrial activity: in setting impossible goals, mankind has created a self-imposed energy shortage for which there exists as yet no safe, non-exploitative, universally equable solution. Local, short-lived bonanzas such as Alaskan and North Sea oil merely buy a little time and help to take our minds off the dilemma.

Chapter Five:
Cities in peril

'There are pressures on people to conform from the moment they're born. They don't get a chance to be individuals. I don't believe in staying in cities. I agree there's no alternative for a lot of people and they'll have to stay in them for quite some time. But I don't see where the energy to run cities is going to come from . . . not even for cooking. Nutrition is an amazing area. I'm trying to find ways of keeping a person alive without doing any cooking at all.'

I'm chewing sprouted wheat and mung beans in the corner of a warehouse in central London talking with John Shore. John is a student attached to the Rational Technology Unit of the Architectural Association, which leases the warehouse, and the partitions round this dark corner are his 'office'. John is a survivalist with a grant to study energy conservation and autonomous living. He constantly chides himself for not doing enough: for information unread, ideas unformulated, experiments unfinished and articles half-written. Lean and fidgety, with an inner energy like a powerfully coiled spring, he has discarded most of his possessions and lives as anonymously as possible in a disused garage. His only means of cooking is a salvaged four-inch-long immersion heater stuck in an ordinary mug, though he hopes to use solar heat from a parabolic reflector whenever he can. The beans and wheat are chewy but sweet, and I learn that by eating them sprouted I'm enjoying up to a hundred per cent increase in vitamin content. 'Some food just has to be cooked,' he admits, 'so

I've got all those Thermos flasks and I'm trying to cook things with just them and this tiny heater.'

Before he moved to the garage, John lived for 18 months in a semi-autonomous portable dome he built himself. There, besides getting turned on to raw food, he designed an aerobic composter toilet and began growing food in boxes. 'The idea is to put the soil from the boxes back in your composter toilet so that now and again it goes through the cycle,' he explains, and he shows me the composter toilet: from outside it looks like an outsize chemical closet with a temperature dial on the side, but under the seat is a heat-insulated container which receives not only faesces and urine, but all compostable material from kitchen and growing boxes. An air inlet and an exhaust vent pipe provide air circulation. If the contents heat up enough, aerobic biological decomposition kills harmful bacteria within eight days, and the compost can be quickly returned to the growing boxes. If not it must be stored for up to a year. 'We've been bringing soil up from Kent in the back of cars so we can continue the experiment with the growing boxes here on the roof. I'm sorry I had to leave the dome, because that's where it all started: I had to find some way of recycling the waste – though normally I never call it waste at all. I prefer to call it a by-product.'

I leave John Shore to catch up with his reading and thread my way through the choking traffic. 'This is the real world,' I say out loud, to test myself. 'This is the focus of it all, the whole might of human skill and engineering which built Centre Point skyscraper, here above the Underground where I'm now going, and all the other hardware that will one day take their place. But if this is real, John's food boxes, fuel saving, waste saving aren't. You can't accept them both. Someone is sane, someone not.'

Advertisements on the platform tell me all is well. People in the carriage are unconcerned. Headlines on their newspapers shout bad news, but with minor differences it's the same bad news they were shouting 40 years ago. The show goes on. John seems grossly outnumbered. Cities don't collapse . . . or do they?

Above the din of the train something he said keeps coming back: '. . . never call it waste . . .' Why does it seem so significant? By the time the train has reached Shepherds Bush, I glimpse why. Until man came into the world there was no waste. Until we invented waste, everything in the biosphere was used again and again so that life could survive. But this Underground, this London and the energy that went into it cannot be re-used. I see it clearly now: instead of helping to create new life, we are creating waste – billions of tons of it: whether tiny specks of plutonium, towering Centre Point, or mountains of garbage. Meanwhile John up there in the warehouse meticulously puts the compost from his toilet back into his growing boxes, and I hear him saying, '. . . I prefer to call it a by-product.' He seems less outnumbered now.

The question that still nags me though is an old, familiar one: 'How did it all happen?' And although by the time I've reached my front door, I haven't answered the knotty one about 'Where we went wrong', I do have a clue which tells me *how* we have been able to go wrong.

Millions of years ago, remember, all those tons of organic matter slipped away from the system – the biosphere to which we belong – to become what we now call fossil fuel. Within the last 200 years, we have used our ingenuity – and power from the fuel itself – to bring it back again into the system. But when it returned, it did so *through the mind of man*, and in this way it was used, not to create more life, but to destroy it. We have used most – if not all – of it to satisfy neither our own needs nor those of the biosphere. Instead, a few of us have used it to multiply our wants, even at the expense of the needs of the rest of mankind, even at the expense of all life.

The Iconoclasts

For some people a city is a place to *experience*, an exciting place of ideas and stimulation – a place through which to pass without putting down roots. For others it is simply where money can be made: *living* happens somewhere else – in protected oases of 'good addresses' or on its fringes in make-believe countryside. Most citizens, however, live either among the cranes and bulldozers of its heartless centre, in nearby slums and high-rise flats, or somewhere among its featureless suburbs. And, despite the statistics of materialism, for a growing number of them it is a place which no more satisfies their basic needs as fulfilled human beings than it satisfies the biosphere, from which the city extracts its nourishment and into which it pours its waste.

If people are to survive – to live in the kind of city the imposed society has built – they must become conditioned to it, as Kit Pedler has expressed. If contemporary society is sick, it is from the city that the sickness stems. A minority manage to break free of the conditioning, however: some to alleviate the distress around them, others to experiment, either individually or in groups, in an effort to create new forms of social organisation. It is among these experimenters that the survivalists are to be found: seeking new ways of working and living together, taking a fresh look at education, working out alternative technologies, and evolving new political structures – some along the lines of the Life Centre and the Movement for a New Society in the USA, others in ways more appropriate to where they are.

Peter Harper aptly describes the alternatives to existing industrial institutions as 'communities of equals without hierarchies, relating as people rather than as roles'. He sees them as small, and with maximum independence of the surrounding economy so that a real price system may be developed – if prices are to be used at all – to demonstrate that an alternative is feasible. 'This favours labour-intensive processes, the use of scrap materials and simple tools, scrap technology, recycling, sharing, "making do" and making "making do" fun,' he says.

In Sheffield one group of people is trying to do just this. In 1971 its founder members bought three houses and a 1,300-square-foot workshop in a working-class district of the city, partly to experiment in shared accommodation, but more to fulfil ideas for a workers' controlled workshop or factory. The group called itself RadTech-in-Pact and set about 'getting together'. It sought to combat what it saw as some of urban society's most serious problems, and from the outset it made its views clear: 'People are faced with a situation where they have relatively little control over their own lives. Their real control over their work is cut virtually to nil by the organisation and ownership of their workplace, by hierarchy, bureaucracy, mystification of skills and qualifications, serving purposes far from those of the workers and people.' The group believed that work was not the only place where this happened: people had become processed as consumers and isolated into nuclear families where the breadwinner was usually the only member of the family who had contact with the work that went on outside the home. This helped to put each person in a constricting category and lessen his sense of responsibility. The group wanted to take a hard look at the many influences over people's lives which they could not understand and so felt incapable of criticising. 'These influences mystify because people trust them, yet they wither curiosity and enable people to accept their powerlessness,' the group emphasised, and it saw professional managers and white-coated scientists as some of the principal 'mystifiers'.

RadTech-in-Pact planned to put some of their ideas into practice by restoring and equipping the workshop. While it took steps to add more people with practical skills, it would embark on some pilot projects. Scrap technology seemed a promising field in which to work: the local community would be involved in collecting it as well as using it; recycling would help reduce the ecological offence of waste-dumping; and the whole idea seemed an inexpensive way to get the workshop humming. Among members of the group, electronics was a major skill, and they hoped to develop uses for the components of discarded radios, TVs and so on, such as intercommunication for elderly people and others who were isolated in their homes.

However, it soon became clear that, although RadTech-in-Pact attracted plenty of interest and visitors, people with skills who were willing to do a real job of work were harder to come by and community involvement was not much easier. The group felt convinced that people to help were around if only they could be found. They published *In the Making*, an annual directory which would put groups and individuals of all kinds in touch with each other – in the country as well as the city. In 1973 progress towards its goal was helped by a £500 prize when it won a competition, 'The Alternative Society Ideas-Pool', but the comfortless appeal for recruits continued: 'We don't have the whole range of skills and experience that we need – but we do have some facilities. We are looking for people who lack facilities, who have skills and general sympathy with our ideas.' Even a year later the group told me: '. . . The proportion of people wanting to write to us, interview us, record us or do research on us is a bit nauseating compared with . . . people willing to do concrete work, to make radical technology work and worker control real.'

A glance through the pages of *In the Making* shows that in 1973 some 15 other groups and individuals in Britain were either setting up industrial-community ventures or seeking people to join ones already started. Two of them aimed to employ useful people rejected by society; several were revitalising crafts; several more using scrap material; and one venture wanted to make shoes that *fit* feet – instead of the reverse. All were on a basis of full worker participation – some living together as well as working together – and all had in common the concept of a more humane urban environment in which people took precedence over machines and money-orientated efficiency.

Similar criteria govern the entries in another alternative directory – *Uncareers*. Two people in Birmingham, Martin and Ann, produce it with volunteers – also unpaid – in their spare time. They question, as they put it, 'the notion that to "find a job", working for someone else, is the best way to get involved in something you care about and like doing. People often feel unhappy about the career world, and find that a regular pay packet is a poor compensation for spending your life like that, but they don't know any alternatives.' As the directory's Introduction says, such work usually means surviving on a lot less money than one would get by working for a well-off organisation. As some compensation for this, projects which qualify for entry in *Uncareers* must treat people as more or less equal, pay nobody a great deal more than anyone else, exploit no one, and discourage people with skills from using them to create a privileged position. A circulation which fluctuates between 300 and 500 each issue generates over 3,000 enquiries direct to the publishers – quite apart from an unknown number of applications direct to the hundred or so projects listed.

The people involved in such ventures represent the 'radical' stream of the alternative society – that which approximates most to the label 'survivalist'. But a parallel movement with less radical aims has already achieved modest success: the Industrial Common Ownership Movement, which in 1974 had ten member firms with a total turnover of nearly £10 million. The Movement's objective is to achieve democratic control of their own work by people at work. It aims to foster experiments, start new firms, and promote the whole idea. It has set up a non-profit-making revolving loan fund to provide finance to would-be ventures. It scorns token action such as putting workers on boards of companies, issuing them with a few shares or either profit sharing or capital sharing. 'We stand for worker control, but a responsible control that is based on ownership,' the Movement proclaims. Its long-term political aim is to see legislation which would make common ownership the basis for all British companies.

One of its foremost pioneers is Ernest Bader, in Northamptonshire, who took 31 years to build up his own prosperous, medium-scale business – 161 people, yearly sales turnover £625,000, net profit £72,000 – and then gave it all away to his workers! Believing in a philosophy which tried to fit industry to human need – rather than the conventional opposite – he transferred ownership of the firm to the Scott Bader Commonwealth in which former employees became partners. The Commonwealth adopted a constitution which distributed power to its members; limited the size of the firm to around 350 people; limited the differential between least and most highly paid to 1 : 7, before tax; restricted grounds for dismissal to 'gross personal misconduct'; made directors fully accountable to the members; split profit between members and outside charities, and forbade sales of its products – polyester resins and allied products – for war-related purposes.

In 1951, when the transfer began, critics were quick to predict that a firm based on collectivised ownership, hampered by self-imposed restrictions, could not survive. But it did. By 1971 annual sales had grown to £5 million, profits to nearly £300,000, and staff to 379. Over the twenty-year period bonuses of over £150,000 were distributed to staff, an equal sum to charities, and several more worker-owned firms were set up.

One of these is Trylon, also in Northamptonshire, a group of 20 people making glass fibre moulds, polyester resins and plastics materials for education. Company objectives are decided by its members, none of whom either contributes to its working capital on joining or takes any if they leave. Virtually all the money borrowed in 1968 to make the switch was repaid in four years, after which the company became self-financing. One of Trylon's concerns is to make work a more fulfilling experience – an end in itself rather than a means of swelling profits. Job flexibility is kept high: workshop and warehouse members help run art and craft demonstrations for teachers, clerical workers do development work on resins – and the manager sweeps out the passages.

Caring and Coping

As any city grows beyond an optimum size, its problems multiply to match, and an increasing proportion of its citizens will be either appropriated to dealing with them or will elect to do so voluntarily. With a slight stretch of the imagination one can visualise the city of the future as a place where most of its citizens are employed in trying to solve city-induced problems: policing, administrating, 'improving' transport, dealing with health problems, emotional stress, and distress, political, religious, and racial tension, unemployment . . . the career and hobby opportunities are endless!

To cope with city-induced problems, the 'welfare' institutions are already over-stretched and demonstrably inadequate, and alongside them, to fill the gap, a host of other community-based alternative institutions are springing up: food co-ops, swap centres, free clinics, free schools, day-care centres, free legal advice centres, free information centres, squatters' organisations, community and 'underground' newspapers and magazines, the Samaritans, local amenity groups, claimants unions, pressure groups and communes.

In London, one organisation seeking to make city life more humane is Gentle Ghost, an association of young people who have come together in a condemned building to find work in which they relate to people *as people*, not merely as mere embodiments of economic functions. 'We are trying to work towards a society of caring individuals, and therefore apart from our usual services are prepared to work very cheaply for people in genuine need,' they declare. Their dilapidated small removal vans, floweringly air-brushed 'Gentle Ghost', are a familiar sight in West Kensington, but less well-known are their other services: architecture, art and design, dressmaking, photography, cooking, decorating, gardening, printing, teaching, translation and Yoga. For young people, who find the establishment alien, Gentle Ghost is a means of doing useful work, sharing their skills, and helping, not only each other, but others around them. The organisation advertises regularly; to cover running expenses it charges its members a commission on the money received for each job they do.

It is a brave attempt, and functions – though not without imperfections: less skilled members complain that skilled ones hoard, rather than share, their experience, and so hog the best-paid assignments; some workers use it unashamedly as a means to build customers, only to drop it as soon as possible to avoid paying commission; sometimes work done is below professional standards; workers do not always turn up. Such shortcomings highlight a feature of the alternative that many in it ignore: 'straight' society may pollute, mystify and exploit, but the hurly-burly of competition can be a spur to doing work to high standards, delivered on time.

Not far away from Gentle Ghost's headquarters is BIT, a 24-

hour-a-day, 7-day-a-week, mostly-free information and help service, open for use by almost anybody for almost any purpose, although, as BIT itself says, 'The aim is to build up alternatives to the present oppressive society and to keep people in touch with hopeful new developments.' One room within BIT's headquarters is open every day except Sundays for people under 'emotional or mental stress' who need someone to talk to – who can give advice on straight or alternative psychiatry. It is staffed and run by Cope, a non-capitalist, anti-psychiatry group, begun in 1973, run on a shoestring, but with hopes of spreading throughout the country. Within the first year it had acquired a house for use as a short-stay crisis centre and a room elsewhere for administration and to handle phone enquiries. They say, 'We hope that the office will also become a sort of research centre and we're collecting some amazing literature in this connection. Our first publication will be a pamphlet on *Coping with the Mental Health Act* – all the stuff the police, shrinks, and hospitals wouldn't tell you. Meanwhile we have our very own quarterly magazine, *Copeman*, which is free to mental patients and 15p to others. Some of us are doing encounter groups run free for us by Quaesitor, and we hope to run our own free or almost free groups sometimes.' In an appeal for helpers, Cope says, 'We can't offer you much money – we've just become a charity and are hassling like crazy to get bread from large trusts to pay our full-time house workers a living wage – about £7. The rest of us only get occasional expenses so we draw Social Security, or if we're sufficiently crazy get a sick certificate, or do odd work. If you're actively interested in anti-psychiatry – or want to be – and are able to get off your ass and work in an unstructured environment for almost no money, meet a lot of people who share those interests, then contact us.'

Alternative organisations, however, are no longer confined to London. In cities and towns throughout Britain, shoe-string operations deal with problems such as drugs, alcoholism, despair, homelessness, unemployment, police brutality, racial discrimination, loneliness and homosexuality, giving free or nearly free advice, professional help, practical help, and genuine caring.

Over in Holland, a wide range of alternative institutions has been linked by a network called the 'Kabouters' ('elves') which, in effect, creates an alternative community within existing society. The Kabouters have set up local action groups and a 'civil service', with 'departments' of agriculture, education, and ecology – they even run an alternative stock exchange. On Amsterdam City Council they have had no less than five representatives. They are active squatters on a large scale, and they run centres for children and old people. In the country they have organic farms selling directly to the network's own low-cost city shops.

Paris has been swept by a wave of communal living among its young people. Ever since the 1968 uprising, the seeds of the movement have been germinating, and recently they have grown rapidly. Their growth has been partly forced by the shortages of satisfying work for young people and living space they can afford; but it is also self-induced, for the new way of living has a liberating quality which attracts more of them to join. Their communes do not necessarily have a clear-cut objective: they are simply places where people live together, sharing what they have and reducing their needs to a minimum – sometimes almost to zero. Members bring in any money they need by going out to work. They find their stimulation, not through commercial entertainment, not by acquiring status and possessions, but simply by interaction among themselves – *from people*.

Some see the commune movement as a quaint, permanent piece of social scenery, strictly for the lunatic fringe; some acknowledge its rapid growth, but look on it as a fleeting phenomenon; others take a different view. One who is optimistic about the movement's future is Keith Hudson in Coventry. In 1972 he launched a monthly journal of survival policies, *Towards Survival*, which he has run in his spare time. 'I didn't know anything about journalism, editing and so on before I started this,' he told me. 'Perhaps I still don't. I feel it's rather more a matter of life or death as regards our civilisation.' Looking back in history he sees two main processes at work: wider access to, or more efficient use of, planetary resources; and wider and ever-more complex groupings of people in a variety of talent. Looking at the present, he sees large institutions and commercial organisations at the end of their tether. Looking ahead, he sees the commune movement as the *beginnings* of an alternative answer to even more powerful economic successors, because its morality is based largely on the more economical use of resources and it transcends national, cultural, and social boundaries. And even if so far it lacks strong international cooperation, a large number of talented people within it show a great deal of empathy and shared values.

Although the movement began in the country, he believes, it is growing most strongly in towns, where he sees it less as an *alternative*, more as an integrated part of existing society, and with valuable roles to play as industrial societies experience economic downturn. Then, he says: '. . . when unemployment reaches a threshold level we are going to see an explosive increase in urban living experiments of a communal nature – for sheer economic survival.' And from these bases he sees talented people emerging to provide leadership during the transition to social change.

Whether in London, Paris, or a smaller city, the fully conditioned urban dweller, working, commuting, living in relative affluence inside the system, has little knowledge of the growing alternative network under his feet: a reaction both to the problems of city living and to the failure of official and conventional charity organisations to win the confidence of people in need. For those who live outside the imposed society – whether from choice or necessity – the network is a lifeline for survival . . . as I found when my journey took me to San Francisco.

Hive or Haven?

This city of hills is not all postcard-blue harbour, the Golden Gate, jolly cable cars, Chinatown and flashy earthquake-defiant skyscrapers. San Francisco has its other sides, and one of them is a district of slab-like warehouses, gaunt, soulless and unloved. After walking the wide, grid-plan streets, weighed down by my back-pack, I enter one of the warehouses through a narrow side door: I am in Project One, a workers' collective in a rambling warren of the antiquated, five-storey building which houses this village within the city. Some 90 people live and work in the building; another 30 live outside but come in to work. Each person living here pays rent for his living space, calculated according to the number of square feet he occupies, plus a standard levy. Each person designs his living space according to his whims and needs. People working together tend to group their living spaces together; they share communal living areas for cooking, eating, and relaxing. Everywhere the psychedelically-inspired décor softens and hides the functional concrete bones of this one-time warehouse.

No commitment to any ideology binds the people to the place. They are inside because they do not feel free outside – here there is no oppression: decisions are made by concensus; so long as a Project One member pays his rent and harms no other member, he may do as he wishes. But he cannot just wander in off the street: he must join one of the existing enterprises or have a viable idea for starting a new one – that is, if space is available. The building houses a wide variety of crafts, businesses, professions, and community-orientated services.

I had met a member of Resource One in London. Resource One is the collective's most glamorous enterprise: the computer, donated as a tax write-off by a large corporation, is now harnessed to serving the community. I learn that my London contact has left the collective, but another Resource One member makes me welcome, and I gladly accept his offer of part of his space as a 'crash pad' during my stay.

The warehouse hums with activity, but seldom jars. The list of other activities is varied: there is a recording studio for pop groups and another which produces programmes on issues of interest to minorities for listener-supported radio stations; a film studio makes use of 16mm government surplus; and nearby 'Optic Nerve' makes videotapes on controversial issues; there is an architects' collective called 'Alternative Structures'. A healing co-op practises massage, hypnotherapy, chiropractics. A lone flautist makes flutes which he sells on the streets; a workers' collective does outside construction jobs; there are freelance musicians and writers, a silk-screening studio, a crafts co-op, a pottery, a sculpture studio, a feminist orientated karate studio; 'Peoplesmedia' give advice to community groups and others on starting and running underground newspapers and magazines; a print shop prints some publications on a salvaged offset-litho press. A day-care centre looks after seven or more children. A favourite of the whole place is 'Symbas', a free school: Project One members teach Symbas teenagers, and where possible encourage them to participate in their own ventures.

To stay at Project One is disorientating. The city recedes and so do its violence, competitiveness, dual standards, and the way it divides life into separate compartments. In here, property rights become blurred. Time takes on a different meaning. Work and living intermingle: work happens when people feel like it – for some right through the night. Leisure is equally flexible. Someone who has not yet gone to bed is having supper next to an early riser eating breakfast. Hierarchies merge. People react to each other, conflicts are explored, and it is hard to pretend. There are plenty of meetings which tend to drag on and on, but since efficiency and money are not the main issues, the subjects get explored in depth, and many conflicts are either resolved or avoided.

Project One, not surprisingly, has its fair share of problems, and one of them has been its relationship with the City Fathers. In general it is tolerated with a kind of possessive pride – as a bourgeois family, out to impress, might carefully let slip mention of one of its harmless eccentric members. And so visiting VIPs are often shown round this 'meaningful social experiment'. So long as the project escaped publicity and notoriety all was well, but before long bureaucracy found that it offended zoning, fire, and health regulations: for a while the cost of a mandatory sprinkler system alone threatened its whole future.

The greater threat, to its future however, is from within. Deep in the highly conditioned American psyche is the urge to achievement and to make money – and when the communards channel too much of their energy into their business ventures, too little is left for Project One. It becomes hard, if not impossible, to get people to work on maintaining the building and administering the project. Attendances at meetings are too low. Symptomatic of the problem was one notice which I saw pinned to a door in one of the corridors: 'The 4th floor show room leaks and floods the bathroom. The 3rd floor toilet hasn't worked since July. The purpose of this notice is not to encourage anyone to *fix* the stuff, but rather to get everybody to feel upset and discouraged and pissed off and guilty so we can hold a meeting and appoint a committee which will hold another meeting and argue and . . .'

I found that people like each other, but they are not 'together' as a community. The various ventures may be viable, but for those who poured their souls into starting the whole experiment, this is not enough: for them Project One, as it has evolved, *proves* too little.

When I eventually met the London contact who had first told me about Project One, she told me just why she had left: 'In the beginning, when the first wave of people were building a home, the community had high spirits,' she said, 'but for the next wave something was missing: they were merely building on something begun by others. It was not *their* dream, not even a dream at all, but a kind of job, an escape, or haven – and when the bureaucrats began threatening, not even a safe one it seemed.' Then the lack of aims became all too starkly apparent: 'Like rotting piles exposed for the first time when the tide goes out,' she said sadly. 'Project One was a beautiful dream. Now it is just a collection of people sharing facilities and paying rent.' When I asked where the idea had begun to go wrong, she felt that there had been too little discrimination in admitting people, too ready an acceptance of a belief that all people were equal when obviously they were not – there were differences in ability, in charisma, energy, affection, and in financial resources. It was a mistake to pretend that these differences didn't exist.

As I reflected on her diagnosis, it seemed to me that what has happened at Project One is symptomatic of the whole alternative movement, in America, Britain, or elsewhere. The imposed society is clear on its aims and commitments to profits, exploitation, and growth, whereas the alternative is unclear about *its* aims: its members are not equally committed. Over time, any institution or system has a need for growth of some kind if it is to hold together. No doubt many who hammer away at the concept of 'the growth economy' are aware of the psychological pay-off – quite apart from the dollar one. Project One's problem was that it had stopped growing – in numbers because the building was full, and ideologically because it had lost its way. It had become diverted into an imitation of the very system to which it claimed to be an alternative.

Nevertheless it would be ill-considered to write off Project One as a failure. Despite its shortcomings it clearly offered its members the opportunity to satisfy their basic needs in a way that the imposed society could not match. Its members did share a sense that they belonged to a place which offered them security as well as some control over the substance of their lives. Love and friendship were apparent – I met no one who confessed to being lonely. Problems they had, but mostly on a scale which was understandable; and for those problems which lay beyond that scale, the help of others who cared was never very far away. By building their own living spaces moreover, they had escaped from the total stranglehold of urban impotence.

The Lethal Magnet

The city of the affluent industrial state is a place which fulfils the needs of only a minority of its inhabitants. By conditioning the majority to accept its shortcomings, it teaches them to tolerate the kind of life it offers. The rest, it largely neglects. Whilst the city reduces the surrounding countryside to the status of a food factory, it spews its industrial waste into the air, dumps it on the land, and – along with human waste – pours it into the rivers and seas. Citizens employed in industry and its administration find themselves spending more and more time and money trying in vain to cope with the problems generated by such a scale. In short: the bigger the city, the less fit it is for people.

To maintain the unwieldly structure requires a continuous input of energy, either directly as food and fuel or indirectly as materials – for materials consume energy to mine, to manufacture, and transport. Each year this complex input becomes increasingly vulnerable: to temporary and prolonged shortages of food and materials; to the inefficiencies of scale; in the breakdown of institutions; to floods and droughts; to strikes, sabotage, and war. It is able precariously to keep going by using technology to solve the problems created by technology. Its industries inhibit solar radiation, disturb the sensitive filters of natural cloud, and artificially raise the temperature of the air. At the same time their effluents poison land and water, threatening the vital process of photosynthesis and interrupting the food chains which support all life. The needs of the major industrial city and those of the biosphere are incompatible!

The city of the affluent industrial state has problems. To retain a sense of proportion, however, consider those which beset the cities of the Third World. Some 300 million people in the Third World now live in cities; during the next 25 years the number will have grown more than three-fold – about half the increase from births in families already there, the rest from people migrating from the countryside in search of work. In most Third World countries the unemployment rate stands at around 30 per cent. Faced with this reality the country dweller turns to the city. Where he is, there is nothing, but in the bustling city he sees some hope; and so, helped by relatives who have preceded him, he moves his family into a makeshift camp or shanty town. In this way rural unemployment becomes urban unemployment.

The city which unwillingly receives him, however, has nothing to offer: no work, no home, no hospital, no school, no transport, no electricity, no sanitation. And so long as every vacant job generates a hundred or more applicants, the hope he brought with him slowly dies. Yet in the city he must still be fed, and so every able-bodied victim like him is one less person to grow the food the city needs. In consequence its endemic shortage steadily worsens.

The conventional solution, adopted by the governments of over-developed and under-developed nations alike, is aid for the cities – to provide essential services and to create jobs. Many, survivalists, however, think differently. As Dr. E. F. Schumacher, author, economist and adviser on rural development problems, has said, you get cities with a rich, modernised section and a vast decaying rural economy, with no bridge between them: 'The implicit theory behind fostering development in Nairobi or Bombay is that you will make a lot of wealth for the ultra-modern units and that this will percolate down to the masses. But all the evidence shows that it doesn't – the duality of the system merely becomes more pronounced.'

Most development aid is the wrong sort – capital-intensive rather than labour-intensive. It simply channels more power and goods to those who already have enough. Every time a new factory is mooted in the city, word promptly goes out to the country and more people come in – far more than the project can hope to employ. Far from solving the problem, such city development only worsens it. The survivalists maintain that the answer lies in creating work *out in the country*, using existing skills and materials and applying alternative technologies appropriate to the ecology and social system of the district.

Chapter Six:
Countryside in need

If I pick up a handful of good soil, squeeze it and then open my fist, the soil separates, but it does not fall apart: it rests, crumbly but intact, upon my spread fingers. But if I try to do the same with poor soil, it either remains one heavy inert lump, or it runs away like sand between my fingers until my hand is empty.

The handful of good soil is a miracle. It is teeming with life – small and invisible, large as a juicy worm. It is rich in humus, and upon this the living creatures feed, releasing naturally the minerals locked inside, in just the quantities that plants need. It is a natural system. Once it had been no more than dead rock: to become this living miracle took perhaps a million years. Treated well by man, it will support life almost indefinitely, demanding nothing but the sun's warmth and the rain's moisture. Treated unkindly by man, it dies within a few generations.

Upon this handful of soil our survival depends. Husband it, and it will grow our food, our fuel, and our shelter, and surround us with beauty. Abuse it, however, and we must force-feed it continuously with chemicals – made in factories from scarce fossil fuel – for it to support life at all. Then, however, it is no longer a natural system: to maintain some kind of balance, to stay firm to hold erect a tree or a stalk of wheat, to withstand drought, flood and wind, it becomes dependent on the calculations of man. But if his calculations are faulty, if the computer is programmed badly or it is fed the wrong data, the soil will collapse and die, taking man with it.

A healthy soil needs a healthy countryside. It needs the husbandry of men and women who understand it, and will care for it, who are close to it, knowing the difference between this valley and that, who are responsive to the seasons, the weather, and the presence of animals, birds, and insects. Machines – whether computers or tractors – cannot replace people. And yet this is exactly what is happening all over the world. In Britain, for example, small farmers have been paid up to £1,000 an acre to sell out to agribusiness – to companies whose aim is to acquire more and more land which they can farm with more machinery and fewer men, making more profit per acre, yet growing *less* food.

Throughout the world the countryside has become a place to be considered essentially in city terms: food factory; playground; receptacle for factory sites, overspill towns, and holiday homes, dormitory suburbs, airports, and motorways. It is a place from which to migrate to the city: young people no longer wish to live there; families, who once earned their livings from the land and from local crafts and industries, are replaced by long-distance commuters, tourists, and couples in retirement.

All of this is entirely understandable and predictable. The city has become the magnet: to live as far from the uncertainties and discomforts of 'nature' has become the overriding aim. The effect is government from the centre, voted in by city dwellers essentially to look after their interests. The inevitable corollary is blind faith in materialism, industrialisation, science, technology and all the paraphernalia of regulation and administration. Each individual, whether city or country dweller, finds himself increasingly dependent on higher technology and the decisions of remote experts. He has less real control over his environment and his destiny.

The majority of people, conditioned to accept conventional wisdom, cling to policies which accelerate the trend. A small minority, among which can be counted the survivalists, wish to reverse it. They seek to lessen the worship of machines which enslave. They seek instead to remind people that their future lies in preserving the miracle contained within a handful of soil.

Land for the People

For 18 years, John and Sally Seymour had been unsung survivalists, living simply and growing just about all the food for themselves and family, first on 5 acres of sandy land in Suffolk and then on a 62-acre farm which they rejuvenated in Pembrokeshire. When they weren't farming and vegetable-growing, bottling, salting down, curing, brewing and winemaking, Sally was making pots for sale through the local crafts shop and John was writing travel books. Although self-sufficiency was their lifelong resolve, they still had to earn a living and trade with the rest of the world for, as John explained to me, 'we run a clapped-out van and buy the odd clothes. The kids can't go to school dressed in rabbit skins!'

Few people had heard of the Seymours until their book *Self Sufficiency*. It was a modest enough work, professional, practical, humorous, and ruggedly philosophical; and, in some people's eyes, something of an anachronism – 'folksy and out of the way' seemed its likely label, the Seymours' own label for 18 hard-working years. But its authors, besides being painstakingly professional, were also wildly lucky, for their book hit the market at the summit of the energy crisis: in the anxious chaotic months of its early appearance it offered a refreshing alternative to the frustrating uncertainties of city life – it became a publishing success.

Now the Seymours' home-cured hams, elderflower wine and off-beat farming methods have become well known. So too are some of John's views, for early in his book he declared with characteristic emphasis that he wasn't interested in the old pre-industrial self-sufficiency of the illiterate peasant or hunter who knew no better, but in the *post*-industrial kind. As he put it: 'that of the person who has gone through the big-city industrial way of life . . . and wants to go on to something better.' He subscribed, moreover, to the view that 'the whole great fragile edifice of global interdependence' could collapse, bringing down the industrial system with it, and he believed that, whether this happened or not, it made far more sense for people to live in the country where they could practise their crafts and grow their own food as well – if they were so minded.

Less well known, however, have been his views on the wider issues of survival, and when I met this stocky, forceful individualist one warm spring day the following year, he told me something about them . . . and stamped himself in my mind as even more a survivalist than I had imagined.

'We're as self-sufficient in food as any people in this country,' he said of his farm and family. 'A few things we buy in, but we grow our own wheat, we make our own bread, we grow our own barley and malt it, we grow our own hops and make our own beer. We're not vegetarians – we have our own beef, mutton, pork, lamb and bacon, continental-type sausages that keep, all our own dairy produce – cheese, butter, buttermilk . . . and we use a lot of honey. Why we do it, I'm not sure, but we've been doing it for years and we're certainly not going to stop doing it, because we like doing it. It's great fun. We work damn hard, but we're working for ourselves, not for somebody else. We never do the same job for more than an hour or two or three, because there's so many different ones that we never do any one long enough to get bored.

'Whether it's desirable that many people should live like this is a very deep, difficult question. Personally I should say "No". I think we're far too self-sufficient – we've made a bit of a fetish of it. Also we've been *forced* to do it because the infrastructure of a regionally self-sufficient economy is not there.' And to make his point he told the story of bread – made of imported wheat, milled in one place, baked in another, sliced, wrapped and delivered – a tasteless, low nutrition product, which had ousted the local baker selling a better loaf made from locally-grown, locally milled wheat. 'An economist would tell you this is a good thing. He'd say you get economy of scale: it's cheaper to have a huge mill in Avonmouth and a huge baker in Cardiff. But the economist is interested in one thing and one thing only, and that's money. He will *always* go for the biggest unit – whether flour mill, textile mill, factory, or farm. The blind workings of the market will always do this. But we're not blind, and I don't see why we should be led by the 'blind working of the market'. We should use our eyes and brains and decide what is best for us, not only from the point of view of money, but also from the point of view of a good life, and healthy communities, both urban and rural.

'The community in the village where I live is being completely emasculated and gutted by the fact that we haven't got any industry there. What was there is dead, and it's become a place where tourists come in summer; in winter it's empty except for people hanging on waiting for the next summer and more tourists to fleece. This is degrading, demoralising, and it doesn't make for good communities.

'I don't think one should ever use the word "efficiency" without saying efficiency for what. Your economist, going for one large city mill instead of small ones scattered throughout the country, is only thinking of money; but if you bring in other factors like social, mental, and physical health, happiness – all sorts of things the economist hasn't been trained in and has never been asked to consider – you get a different answer. Our economists and businessmen should consider these other answers, or we should kick 'em out and try to work out our answers without them.'

It was beyond his power to re-start local wheat growing or milling, so he simply practised it on his own farm, he explained. 'The local farmers have been sold body and soul to this idea of specialisation, and the thing they do is *produce milk*. They put churns of milk on the road every day and a lorry comes along and takes the milk away. If they want a cabbage they buy it at the greengrocers – it comes from Covent Garden, believe it or not. Two 18-ton articulated lorries full of cabbages come down every day to Fishguard and on to Cardiff. This is specialisation, economy of scale and all the things economists love. But cabbages grow very well in Pembrokeshire, and if you buy them from Covent Garden there's something very sick about it.'

He maintained that there was enough land in the country for

anyone to do what he was doing *and* send surplus food to the towns and cities, but the trouble was that the land had been grabbed. 'It was grabbed in 1066 and it's been held ever since by the people who grabbed it then, or the people they've sold it to. Why should Lord So-and-so own 18,000 acres in the Home Counties when another man doesn't own an acre? Is this fair and equitable?' He explained that the establishment's answer was always that it was more efficient to farm land in large units. Obviously a farmer with a thousand acres made more money than one with a hundred acres or two acres, but what mattered was not the amount of profit got from each acre but the amount of food; and in that respect the small acreage was *always* more efficient.

'I've got 62 acres, but in fact I'm only self-sufficient on about 10 of them, which we farm intensively: the rest we sort of "dog and walking stick" farm with a flock of sheep, some cattle and ponies. My 10 acres produce more food to the acre than our neighbouring farmer's 200 acres. It's because we put more labour into them. But economists would say it's nonsense, because our expenditure of labour is high – it's labour they're trying to save, the most expensive factor in anything these days. So they say "knock ten 100-acre farms into one, save labour and make more profit per acre". You will – but you'll grow less food. Economists will then tell you that ten families were eating the food, but now there's only one and so there's more net production. But they forget that the nine families they've kicked off have got to live somewhere, probably in some city, so you don't get any saving in fact.'

John Seymour normally thinks and talks fast, but he made the next point slowly to let it sink in: 'If every 10 acres of this country were farmed the way I farm my 10 acres on which I'm self-sufficient, we wouldn't have to import any food from abroad at all!'

In England and Wales there was up to three-quarters of an acre of arable land per head – including babies; and in addition there was rough grazing which could produce plenty of meat and milk, he maintained. 'This is enough land – the Chinese could feed a population at least double ours on it. We could too, but not on 1,000-acre farms with one man sitting in a cab on a tractor going up and down, up and down. Our agriculture has become entirely dependent on imported protein, oil, and fertiliser. Our huge grain farms would grow nothing without enormous applications of sulphate of ammonia – and it takes 10 tons of coal equivalent to produce every ton of it. Our protein comes from fish meal or crops like soya beans from tropical countries, and if this dried up we'd be in a terrible muddle – I think we'd starve.' He believed that we should experiment with growing protein in Britain, but this was only possible on the small, labour-intensive farm, not geared to monoculture. On such a farm it was possible to be independent of imported fertilisers. 'On our place we have tons of manure. We don't use chemicals because we don't need them; as far as fertility is concerned we're a self-supporting unit. It was an absolutely derelict farm when we came here, and in 10 years we've turned it into a highly fertile place. Every year you can see our land getting better and better.

'People have to start farming to a certain extent with human muscle again. I have a tractor – one was going cheap – but if it disappeared tomorrow it wouldn't alter our way of farming – I've got a couple of horses. If the price of fuel goes up a few more notches I'll soon dump it. I'm not against intermediate technology, such as tractors, but we shouldn't allow tools to override us. The tractor's there and I'm its boss – it's not *my* boss. Once you get to the state where you're absolutely dependent on machines – as commercial farmers are nowadays – you're in a very poor state. If there really was a shortage of oil in this country again I think we would all starve because it would be impossible to grow any food at all.'

John and Sally Seymour have given much thought to how they could better use their under-farmed 52 acres. They would be willing to bring in five more families and either run it on some communal basis, or else divide it into six units, possibly with each family having 5 acres and communal use of the remainder. There is one impediment, however: the planning laws. As John says bitterly: 'You can't do any kind of experimenting with alternative ways of living. When I put in my application to divide up my farm, all my neighbours supported me. They didn't mind if we started a community and the people had beards and long hair. They didn't care, but the planning people would. . . . I think you'd have an awful lot of trouble with them. They're extremely conventional people who can only understand things they know. We should bash away on the political level to get the planning laws changed.

'I shall never see the sort of countryside I'd like to see, though it may happen in a hundred years' time. I'd like to see lively, varied communities like there were in the eighteenth century, when cities not only *took* from the country but *contributed* as well. Now cities have grown far too big, and they've sucked life out of the country. They're just damn great sumps. The trouble is that our governments are always city governments because most of the voters live in cities, therefore they're not really interested in the land.'

A Little Piece of Land
Even before I set off on my long journey into the Alternative, the idea of self-sufficiency was very much in my mind. If one felt oppressed by the size of cities and their institutions, if one was conscious of less and less control over one's life, self-sufficiency seemed the ultimate answer. I encountered on the way many who felt likewise – including the Seymours, the Mansons, the Vales. I met others too in the United States – in Connecticut, North Carolina, Florida, and New Mexico. Everywhere I went, I found the same motives and attitudes: revulsion of a system which pretends to liberate people while it enslaves; a turning away from bigness to smallness, away from a preoccupation with machines to concern for people, away from dominating nature to living in harmony with nature. Few people of those whom I met embodied these motives and attitudes more than the De Kornes.

Jim and Elizabeth De Korne live with their two children in an

adobe house near a remote village 7,000 feet up on the southern
Rockies of New Mexico. It is autumn when I call on them; the air
is crisp in the clear sunshine, and the backdrop of rugged mountains is etched sharply against an intense blue sky.

They greet me warmly enough, but I get the feeling I'm being
scrutinised . . . why have I come? . . . what do I want of them?
The place to my eyes is desolate, a lonely place, for people who
want to be left alone. 'I'd like to see what you're doing here,' I
find myself saying rather too obviously.

'It's early days yet, but I'll be glad to show you what there is,'
Jim replies.

We walk round to the back of the house and he shows me five
second-hand wind generators lying in a row. 'I'll keep two,' he
explains, 'one to power a deep-freeze, the other to run a small
water pump I'm going to show you in a minute.' We walk over to
a large concrete block surmounted by a cage with rabbits in it.
He explains how they will be able to build burrows in the soil
inside the concrete base and so live in the most natural conditions
possible. He explains how the young can be ready for eating at
eight weeks, each doe producing 100 lbs of protein a year.

He shows me the cool root cellar he built into the hillside, and
I am introduced to two goats and twenty-three chickens. Although
the De Kornes's land is not rich, with heavy composting and
judicious watering from a communal irrigation ditch they produce more vegetables than they need from their one acre and they
sell the surplus quickly and profitably as 'organically grown' in
Santa Fe market.

He tells me these things with quiet pride, but as we walk to the
other side of the land I sense that he has been saving the best till
last. And I am right. For we come upon the object of his hopes – a
hydroponic greenhouse and fish tank . . . he reels off the descrip-
tion laconically enough, but his excitement shows through. It's a
long, low-built greenhouse, and we enter through a trap door and
down steps until we are below ground level – and several degrees
warmer. 'This 1,400-gallon tank at the front here will have cray-
fish and catfish growing in it,' he explains. 'A wind generator will

charge a battery to run a pump which will circulate the tank water through a flat-plate solar collector. As it returns to the tank it will pass through a filter to trap the algae and other nutrients, and then across a piece of slate so that it falls through the air and is re-oxygenated. To feed the fish I'll raise angleworms which eat compost, kitchen refuse, manure, and grass cuttings. Angleworms are a kind of earthworm, but they breed better and multiply faster, and their castings are the best compost known to man. I'll put the castings into 55-gallon drums with holes punched in the bottom, and the water which is leached from them will feed vegetables growing in hydroponic tanks. They will grow in gravel, and the hydroponic solution will provide all the nutrients they need. Hydroponics with chemicals is routine, but, to my knowledge, I'm the first one to try it with organic nutrients – I don't want to be dependent in any way on the outside culture for any of my energy. In winter we get sunny days and very cold nights, but the solar collector will heat the water, and during the night the body of water will radiate its heat and keep the temperature up. Five hundred dollars is all I put into it – a guy with a back hoe dug the hole for a hundred dollars, but the rest of the labour was all our own.'

We linger a while until the whole process is made clear, and then Elizabeth suggests we go inside the house and she'll make some tea. On the way back I learn that both of them once had regular jobs, but now they want nothing more than to be left alone out here on the edge of the desert on the edge of the System. When we are indoors and Elizabeth is making the tea, I ask Jim why. It is a full minute before he answers me, and when he does he has sat down opposite me and his eyes are full on me.

'I live here because I can't live anywhere else. I've chosen to dissociate myself from the mainstream of American activity. I sometimes think of the 1 acre that I own as my own little country. And I am king of it. I guess you'd call me an anarchist – "a pox on all their houses". I consider myself an American only by birth – and that was an accident, I could have been born anywhere. I believe that most political activity is a move to get power over others, for your party, for yourself.

'I graduated in 1961 with a master's degree but I had no idea what to do. I only knew there was more to life than making money 5 days a week, and I looked for some meaning in my life.

'I think I'm finding it here. I bought this place in 1967 at a time of crisis in my life. I was teaching, but I wanted to get out of it. Except when I had students who really wanted to learn – almost impossible in a system where kids are forced to go to school – I hated it. I could turn on a few kids but I could never turn them all on. So I decided to go to a photography school in California – photography had always been my hobby, and now I wanted to become a professional. I thought it would be the answer to my life problem because it would give me the independence I needed, and at the same time the work would be creative. But before I set off, I knew I wanted to come back to New Mexico, to a little piece of land. That week I saw an ad in the paper for a house and 1 acre, price $3,000. I came up here, looked at it and I knew I wanted it. I put some money down on it and paid the rest off during the next couple of years.

'I came back and got a job as staff photographer at the Museum of New Mexico. We were living in Santa Fe, but the rent kept on going up, so we moved here and began commuting, but that was a real drag, and one day we said: "We don't need a job any more, we've got enough saved up to live here." So we did.

'Like my neighbour, Peter van Dresser, I don't think one hundred per cent self-sufficiency is possible unless you want to live like a caveman. But I do think that a worthwhile goal for a human being to strive for is a feeling that he can take care of himself and his family. You feel a better human being if you know you don't depend on a whole lot of industry. And the more people who do drop out and achieve a certain measure of self-sufficiency the less profit for the establishment and the military-industrial complex. And I think that's valuable.

'Ideally I would like to see a decentralised kind of economy and culture in this country in which communities provide most of their own things. My experience of "community effort" so far is that I'm the one who provides all the tools and most of the know-how but I don't get a heck of a lot back for it.'

Elizabeth comes in with the tea and for a while we talk on other subjects. Then I ask Jim: 'Out here you're taking plenty from society, but what are you giving back?'

Characteristically he pauses, then looks straight at me again, though this time he is frowning. 'I drive a pick-up truck, and my chain-saw uses gasoline. My greenhouse has fibre glass on it: I can't make it so I have to buy it and this is the real paradox. I'm aware of it all the time and yet I don't know what to do. I could make life really hard on myself – and Elizabeth and the kids – by not having these things, but then I wouldn't accomplish anything either. I hope I can give back the proof that people can live a more meaningful life by taking care of themselves. I want this place to be a showcase for the rest of the world: that the greenhouse I've built, in a 24-foot by 24-foot space of ground, holds forth the possibility of feeding a family of four – and without any chemicals or anything which is bad for ecology – that could be important for the Third World. This is the kind of contribution I can make.'

'But if you are successful with these experiments how are you going to communicate them? It's pretty remote here . . .'

'By my writing. I've written two articles for *Mother Earth News* and I've fifteen or twenty more articles in my head. There are many answers to the problems we have. I'm taking the one that pleases my psyche and I believe that if a number of us begin to do this, then people will say, "Hey, that guy, he's leading a pretty good life," and they'll start doing it too. Like a whole bunch of people over here playing soccer, and a couple of guys say "don't wanna play soccer any more, I wanna play baseball". And so they do. Then the people playing soccer say, "Hey, that looks like it might be more fun than what we're doing," and so, by attrition, they start dropping out. And pretty soon nobody's working for General Motors any more. In my thinking, that's the only way change ever happens.'

I ask Elizabeth if she knew what she was in for when she married Jim.

'I did,' she replies, 'because I knew this place before we moved in permanently. And now we're here, I keep a balance between the housework and work outside. I like the slower pace – it's a question of getting used to it, and when you do it's very satisfying.'

'But don't you feel isolated from other women . . . from ideas?'

'To a certain extent I do, but a family has moved up here from Santa Fe – he was a director of the folk art museum there. They came to an open house we had. It was snowing and the birds were eating seed we'd put out on the window sill . . . they were ecstatic about the whole way we were living. And so he quit the museum and came here, and they are good friends of ours. You really only need a couple of people that you know you can see if you want to. Most of the time we're so busy we don't have an awful lot of time to socialise except in the evenings. Sometimes when people come and just want to sit around we resent it because we have a certain schedule to follow and it's hard to pick a happy medium. It depends largely on the kind of person you are and what you want out of life. This isn't the kind of life for anyone who's even slightly inclined to Women's Lib. I just don't happen to agree with that outlook. Jim and the boys don't do dishes or wash floors, but they have their jobs that I can't do like hauling water.'

'You'd say that a woman must accept the traditional role to live this kind of life?'

'I'd say so.'

Jim chimes in: 'I don't necessarily agree with that. I believe in Women's Lib. The division of labour depends on the people. Some women might want to go out there and lay cement, and I say "great", but Elizabeth doesn't want to. The way the division of labour has turned out here is pretty much the nineteenth-century farm thing. It works for us, but I'd never say that Women's Lib had no place in this kind of life.'

The talk gets around to personal things. I learn about their outside income: that apart from selling surplus vegetables, writing, and a little freelance photography Jim is signed up on fire crews and that every few weeks he goes out to fight a forest fire. In between times he makes simple, Spanish-style furniture which is sold in Santa Fe. Elizabeth gives piano lessons and occasionally types manuscripts, but even so they once ran out of funds and had to shut up the place while Jim went back to the teaching he hated. All this reminds me of that 'certain schedule' and I feel I should be on my way. 'Do you think a society based on alternative values has any chance?' I asked as a parting shot.

'My way of looking at the whole thing is perhaps Darwinian,' Jim answers. 'If a species adapts itself to a certain environment and becomes so specialised that it can only live within that environment, and then the environment changes, it perishes – like the dinosaurs. If a real catastrophe happens and people are suddenly cut off from the things they've gotten used to, then the ones who are going to survive are those who know how to look after themselves. I'd like to think that the people who are doing this are going to be the first wave of a whole new world order of decentralisation . . . one in which there is true peace, in which people know how to cooperate with each other instead of competing in the big power struggle.'

Next spring I hear from Jim. He wasn't able to get the wind generator hooked up to the greenhouse before winter, and so he couldn't cycle water through the solar collector. 'But the water never froze,' he writes, 'even on the coldest nights when outside temperatures reached 10 below zero. We raised lettuce, radishes, spinach, and cabbage through the winter, and now with warmer weather they are growing well. In March we're getting fresh salads from the greenhouse – even though 4 inches of snow fell last night and it looks like more is on the way. I'm overjoyed at how it performs even half-completed.'

He has had rabbit trouble due to cave-ins, he writes. 'I may have to remove the entire roof and really get in there and stomp it down good and hard. Charles Proctor, my ex-boss from the Museum, now has a small homestead across the creek from us. He and his wife have a very successful quilt-making business here. They aren't into the self-sufficiency thing as much as I am, but they are certainly further along than most Americans.'

Community on a Human Scale
In the village of El Rito nearby, Peter van Dresser has a totally different concept of self-sufficiency from the De Kornes, the Seymours, and others. And he is a man for the people of any nation to heed: his ideas are belatedly gaining acceptance across a country so obsessed with getting on that it had never asked where it was going.

Peter van Dresser was speaking and writing about ecology in the 1930s while the highly evocative work was still hidden in the small print of the dictionary. When 'drop-out' was a word yet to be coined, this architect, engineer, and pioneer in non-military rocket propulsion, left these establishment-ridden activities for something which he felt had more relevance to survival. He and his wife, Florence, chose remote El Rito high in the southern Rockies because of its problems. The unique region was culturally rich and naturally well-endowed, but it had a long history of deforestation, over-grazing, soil erosion, river silting, floods, all inevitably leading to declining agricultural production, rural depression, and an ageing outward-migrating population. To Peter and Florence the region offered an irresistible challenge, for they cherished a deep conviction that it could be revived in a way other than conventional federal aid and development programmes – even if such programmes ever effectively reached the people there. Whatever happened, this was an unlikely event, for 'progress' always passed by: as Peter put it in his book *A Landscape for Humans*: 'The statistics remain stubborn, always indicating a reluctance of the regional community to participate wholeheartedly in the general march of industrial and commercial progress.' If his ideas could be found to work in such a place, they could spread to other underdeveloped regions far afield.

The van Dressers settled there to develop a concept they had evolved: one in which naturally defined regions might become self-sufficient through the skills and intelligence of their people, grouped into communities on a human scale. He saw them making use of modern technology, yet existing harmoniously with the natural world around them. The couple decided from the outset to work closely with the villagers. To be part of the community was essential, so, with local materials, they restored an old adobe house, and opened a small roadside restaurant in which they served home-grown food.

When, in the autumn of 1973, we talked together by the wood stove in his homely kitchen, he stressed that he had not come to El Rito as 'an ecological messiah' or reformer with a message of salvation, but as a refugee. 'I needed many of the values that were already historically here in the village . . . things on a human scale,' he explained, 'freedom from the pressures of large-scale commercialism and industrialisation. I did feel I might in time make some contributions to the community, but my main problem was to evolve a personal survival economy which would be relatively non-exploitative and meshed with the local economy. I never believed in the idea of total self-sufficiency, homesteading on some mountain peak or something of that sort.'

With characteristic understatement, he went on to say that he had devoted 'a certain amount of effort' to village community efforts: bringing water to the village, despite one obstacle after another, had been entirely due to his efforts; with a priest and a teacher he had set up a small community school as an alternative to the public school which many of the villagers were unhappy about . . . 'a rich experience while it lasted'.

But his lasting and overriding preoccupation has been his concept of 'biotechnic' development of the region. For this he has sat on committees and government advisory groups, and written reports and papers. His aim has been to create a climate of opinion in which such a development would be recognised as valid for the region. 'All the while, I've operated on a number of different levels, all pushing in the same direction, but the forces which are moulding us in the end are pushing in the other direction. They are so enormous, so cumulative and ubiquitous that nobody fighting them can claim much success. I've kept trying, that's all I can say.

'I live in hope that a genuine psychic change may be operating seriously on society as a whole, and that the present gropings towards an alternative society are the forerunners of a serious movement. But from my experience with it I find it confused, fragmented, and self-defeating.' He went on to criticise communes and individuals who pretended at self-sufficiency, yet still went to Safeways for their proteins. 'There's a middle ground where you don't pretend at self-sufficiency, but rely as much as possible on the resources and products of the local economy.' This he saw as a slow, evolutionary process in which the district tried to reduce its dependence on a greater economy, utilising the products of the region more effectively. He preferred 'recentralisation' to 'decentralisation' as a way of describing this evolution – one which would not involve wholesale migrations from cities, but would happen over a period of decades. The first stage would be a halting of the exodus from rural areas to cities, and a relative shifting of growth rates in favour of smaller centres. '. . . We'd see a re-colonisation of country districts so that they could be reclaimed gradually, gently, skilfully, and artistically . . . a utopian hope, but I still feel it is the only way out of the terrible *impasse* our civilisation is getting into.'

He was well aware of the system's capacity to keep going even though conditions gradually deteriorated; consequently he saw little likelihood of sudden collapse. 'One hopes that by taking thought and by statesmanship we could avoid that kind of solution, and I do think that an alternative lifestyle has at least the germ of a concept for a solution, and for that reason it is very precious. But it is still only a germ – not even an embryo,' he said ruefully. He was interested in a strategy which would bring to the surface in rational terms the undercurrent of feeling so that it could be recognised as a sound understandable solution. 'It does already appeal to many, many people,' he said, 'but they have been so brainwashed with so many traditional teachings and pseudo-economics and so on in schools that they have dismissed such notions as romantic dreams. But they are *not* romantic dreams: they are very practical. There is a great need to discuss these ideas in *rational* terms and show that – as is so often true – an aesthetic feeling is a latent indicator of economic and functional rightness. This is where we're lacking. If such a mode of thinking became widespread, a much greater body of Americans would be interested in this whole movement and would implement it – especially if there was a demonstration that it is not dependent on hallucigenics and pseudo-mysticism.' He paused and I suggested: 'The alternative has an image which deters people who might otherwise move over ...'

'Which actually gets in the way of intelligent thinking on the subject. I haven't come across a single new idea that wasn't discussed in the decentralist movement of the thirties,' he stressed.

When we discussed the role that alternative technology might play in achieving change, he expressed concern that it reflected the typical American hope that gadgets would solve problems: he saw much of the present spate of activity as a status symbol. He argued that it was far more relevant first to change our motivations, and our social and economic relationships; he believed that if we did so, technology would then evolve in a way that satisfied real human needs.

'What we're talking about then,' I suggested, 'is a spiritual change ...'

'Which expresses itself in rather prosaic terms – in the kind of houses we build; in the kind of industries we develop and the goods we trade in,' he added. 'I don't think there is a dichotomy between spiritual and material bases. What we feel is a Christian fallacy that has done so much damage.'

'What do you see as standing in the way of desirable social change?' I asked.

'We have built a Frankenstein monster of industrial and commercial relationships which is almost totally running our lives,' he answered. 'It derives its motivation from our acceptance of it and our failure to conceptualise any other value system. A very subtle subject. The change I'm talking about . . . I don't know how to describe it . . . a psycho-cultural change? I wouldn't call it just a spiritual change, but it would certainly have to include what are called spiritual values.'

Some days later, as I set off on the dusty road out of El Rito and Peter van Dresser shrank into the blue distance, I found myself saddened by the thought of so much wisdom ignored, so much devotion unappreciated, so much life spilled on the parched soil of the region with too little time left for him to see any fruit harvested. From our talks I knew that he nursed deep disappointment: not only for the failure of either the villagers or the bureaucrats to respond to his efforts; but also for the failure of today's 'germ of a movement' to act responsibly. But I knew, too, that he was unshaken in a conviction that one day, a long time off, an inexorable chain of events would precipitate a change in thinking which would prove his philosophies to be right. Then, just as 'ecology' has emerged from the small print to become headlines, so survivalist Peter van Dresser, and his book, *A Landscape for Humans*, would be seen in their true perspective.

The Global Context

The De Kornes and the van Dressers are not so remote from the Mansons and the people of Eithin y Gaer as they might at first seem. If a new movement to achieve social change based on new values is to grow and succeed it is likely to come from thoughtful men and women whose actions attract others to them, and whose message is spread and by those who travel to see them, and by their own writings. They are not necessarily in conflict with the survivalists who choose to remain in the cities. These have a dual role: to make cities more *humane* places, and to seek ways of making them places less in conflict with the needs of the biosphere and so survive. Their task is immense. Throughout history, the world over, the countryside has been bled to nourish the city. There, power has grown: in the hands of government, church, army, landlord, banker, merchant, industrialist, educator, communicator . . . the whole paraphernalia of mysticism and oppression. The flow has been almost entirely one-way, accepted, virtually without question, as Progress and Civilisation. Only now is a small minority of scattered people challenging the morality of this flow and presenting it as a cause – if not *the* cause – of the imminent breakdown of society and the biosphere.

City-based civilisations have traditionally indulged in the luxury of protecting themselves from the vagaries of the natural environment. Successive wielders of power have remained largely deaf to the small chorus of voices which remind them of the greater power, beyond their city walls, on which they finally depend. In the over-developed industrial nations there is little sign that the voices of survivalists seeking to reverse the flow are being heard or their actions recognised; for while machines and money have an almost irresistible fascination, there is no apparent glamour in a fistful of soil. And the picture throughout the rest of the world is little different – with one massive exception: China.

In 1972 Harold Dickinson travelled more than 3,000 miles through China – the whole way by train, so that he could see conditions well away from urban areas. And significantly he found that the drift of population from the land to the city had been reversed. On his return he described the development of the People's Commune as one of the most important social experiments of the present time. 'The division of non-industrial China into 78,000 semi-autonomous communes has provided China with a solution to the problems that also affect other parts of the world,' he wrote.

As he pointed out, China has more than 760 million people, and 80 per cent of them work on the land or in related activities. Ten per cent work in manufacturing industry – steadily expanding, according to plan, away from the traditional pre-liberation areas of Peking and Shanghai and into the rest of the country.

Before 1949 when the People's Republic was established, almost all the fertile land was owned by landlords, many of them absentees. Tenants paid their rents in kind, usually about 50 per cent of total production, but 75 and even 90 per cent were not uncommon levies. In the all-too-frequent bad years, millions starved or fled to other equally impoverished areas. The new régime promptly took land titles from the landlord class and gave them to the peasant cultivators.

At first, small groups of them began sharing their tools and tasks, and in doing so they found they could achieve more. Over the years, the grouping continued, and by 1958 most of the nation's rural population was living in some 78,000 People's Communes, ranging in size from 6,000 to 60,000 people. Each commune was divided into Brigades and Production Teams based on natural villages.

Today, the primary aim of a commune is agricultural self-sufficiency, but it also makes as many as possible of its daily necessities – clothes, shoes, ropes, baskets and so on, and runs workshops to make and repair tools and the simpler kinds of machines. Commune members are paid partly in cash, partly in kind, and each family owns enough land to be self-sufficient in eggs and vegetables, with the right to sell surpluses for cash. Every family owns its house – usually austere – but at least no one is homeless. Specialised teams from the commune build the houses, financed by members' savings.

Although each commune has a high degree of autonomy in day-to-day work, it is connected to the State through Country and Provincial Authorities to ensure that its output conforms to a national plan which attaches great importance to growing grain and protein. To this end, each Province, County, Commune, Brigade, and Team is set a target which it tries to over-fulfil. Harold Dickinson stresses that the communities '. . . provide the individual peasant with a living and working unit which he can comprehend, with which he can identify himself, and in which he has a reasonable chance of participating in management.'

He writes that the mass of the rural population accepts the rule of the Communist Party, which has greatly reduced the possibility of widespread flood or famine, and has provided adequate food, housing, and basic social services. He sees the emphasis on the use of local materials in intensive agriculture as an important lesson in development. 'On a more fundamental level,' he writes, 'the political and ideological bases of modern China grew from the experience of prolonged war and revolution. Such circumstances are unlikely to reoccur elsewhere in the absence of similar social upheavals: there are those who believe that a just society is impossible without such social disruption.'

Chapter Seven:
Something to eat

Trance-like, husbands and wives wheel their trolleys to wall-paper music in the over-bright, air-conditioned ambiance. Layer upon layer of food surrounds them, invisible behind its armour of plastic, metal, and cardboard packaging; but multicoloured labels of tempting portions, healthy, smiling faces, and pastoral scenes convince them the food is there. Everything is *convenient*: 'slit here . . . no fuss, simply add water . . . just heat and serve.' Everything is within arm's reach, made even more tempting by free offers of patio chairs, sunshine holidays, and gift stamps. This is the principal focus of industrial endeavour – the make-believe world of consumer land.

Somewhere outside, a long way away, people labour long in the fields to grow food and cope with temperamental animals, or sail into treacherous waters to catch elusive fish. Their work can be pleasant and rewarding, but because they are generally exploited, and in turn exploit, more often it is not. For them, no air-conditioning: they sweat in blistering heat; shiver in bitter gales or frost. When gales lash the oceans into fury, they catch no fish; when winds blow soil away, the tender crops are exposed, wither, and die. When torrential rain washes the naked, vulnerable soil into swollen rivers, carcasses float over flooded farms. Luckier beasts live on, only to travel miles to be slaughtered, staggering bruised and terrified on the foul, slippery floors of swaying cattle trucks. Calves, pigs, hens live all their lives penned in cages, fed on hormones and antibiotics. Out in the fields, men spray their highly-bred 'artificial' crops with millions of gallons of factory-made poison in an unending battle with pests and diseases. To force the tired land to keep growing crops year after year, machines throw out millions of tons of artificial fertilisers – indeed so much that huge excesses of chemicals filter through the subsoil to poison drinking water supplies, kill fish, and turn whole lakes stagnant. Agribusiness is rapidly ousting the small farmer – a mechanised way of extracting food so wasteful in precious energy that as much as five calories of fuel have to be expended to obtain one calorie of food.

Many of the men and women who grow the food, which comes from far away, cannot keep enough of it back to give their families a varied and adequate diet: strange international economics deny them essential protein so that it may be shipped to industrial nations and fed to cattle, pigs, and hens.

If a consumer should ever feel an urge to brush with reality, he has only to flip through the pornography of the big farming and horticultural magazines. There he will see page after page of advertisements for highly toxic substances and violent, earth-tearing machinery, backed by editorial support, guaranteed to shatter the illusion of his supermarket's pastoral packaging pictures. All this in magazines about the food he will eat!

This is the *real* world outside, which succours the consumer society at the expense of the biosphere. It is not a pretty picture. In the past few years the world's food stocks have become exhausted. The Green Revolution has failed; exceptional droughts and floods – possibly aggravated by industrial man's disturbance to the biosphere – have ruined harvests; over-bred crops have failed to yield their quota, as pests and diseases overtake man's efforts at control. And all the while the world population increases relentlessly at the rate of nearly a million every week.

For any who doubt the seriousness of the problem a little-publicised 1974 United Nations report stated the facts forthrightly and eloquently. Many people believe that, despite periodic local setbacks, world living standards are rising – that people are better fed. By assembling a mass of information from all over the world, the report, *Preliminary Assessment of the World Food Situation Present and Future*, shattered that illusion with one telling blow. Its new estimates put the number of people in the world suffering from malnutrition at 400 million – that is 14 out of every hundred. 'This is not just a cold statistic,' the report said. 'It describes the daily physical privation of fellow human beings, adversely affecting health and physical growth, and seriously reducing the capacity of children to learn and adults to work. This is a conservative statistic . . . a less conservative definition might double the figure.'

In 97 developing countries a *cautious estimate* indicated that no less than half their young children were inadequately nourished – 10 million of them severely so. Of the problem generally, the report stated: '. . . it seems probable that over the past decade the number of persons suffering from malnutrition has actually increased.

For a few more years people in the rich, industrial nations may be able to go on wasting and abusing food and generally over-eating in the manner to which they have become accustomed. They can permit obscene 'mountains' of European butter and beef to accumulate while millions beyond their favoured frontiers starve – as they did in 1973–74. They may do all this for a while longer, but not indefinitely. According to Harold Dickinson, catastrophic famine in India, well within a decade, is almost inevitable. If he is right, the disaster is likely to have two significant effects *outside* India: not only could it signal the total collapse of a system already precariously balanced; it could bypass the workings of the market, the propaganda of governments, the reassurances of 'experts', the fiction of the TV screen, and its agony would directly penetrate the hearts and minds of people everywhere. Conditioned man would wake up to see the make-believe world of his consumer society as having no more substance than the cardboard round his processed food. His conscience would not permit him to remain passive.

Radical Agriculture

The conventional solution to feeding the rising populations is 'the mixture as before' – only more of it. Britain, for example, which is now dependent on the rest of the world for about half her food needs, still confidently expects food to flow in to her ports, despite the population explosion in countries where the food comes from, the impending fertiliser shortage, the spectre of steadily declining soil fertility, and the increasing vulnerability of crops to pests, diseases, and genetic breakdown – both at home and abroad.

The survivalists' approach, in contrast, is to foster *caring* for the countryside instead of exploiting it. This implies an alternative kind of agriculture which is more labour-intensive than capital-intensive. It means one which uses the muscle power of animals and humans to help conserve the vanishing energy resources now powering the farm machinery on which our stomachs become daily more dependent. It involves less reliance on artificial fertilisers and more use of compost, animal and human manure, and of factory and city waste generally. And it rejects the whole concept of monoculture, contending instead that a diversity of healthy crops and livestock grown by caring people on organically enriched soil in the most natural environment possible, holds far more hope for survival than ever-increasing dependence on inbreeding and pesticides.

Throughout Britain, in their different ways, thousands of people are adopting this alternative approach. In the spirit of the Seymours, the Vales, the Mansons, John Shore, and the people at Eithin y Gaer, countless other individuals, in cities, towns, and country, simply in their own gardens or allotments, some as members of organic gardening associations, some in farm-oriented communities, are working towards the same goals. They are part of a world-wide movement which is marrying ancient wisdom with new, alternative technologies in an attempt to grow more food without mortgaging the future.

Such survivalists are no new phenomenon: all that has changed is the problem's size and urgency. One who shared their vision and concern was Henry Doubleday, a Quaker smallholder, who lived from 1813 to 1902. Appalled by the death toll of the Irish potato famine and a possibility of a similar recurrence, he sought a resilient, nutritious and high-yielding crop that would feed a hungry world. He found it – so he believed – in the plant, Russian Comfrey, and this he introduced to Britain, spending the last thirty years of his life in research from which he neither sought, nor received, profit.

Today his work is continued by an association of 3,000 people in many countries. Inspired by its director-secretary, Lawrence D. Hills, the Henry Doubleday Research Association conducts research not only on its two-acre trials ground at Bocking in Essex, but on the farms and gardens of many of its members, who send their findings for collation and publication in the Association's newsletter. But its work today embraces much more than trials with Russian Comfrey – claimed to be the fastest builder of vegetable protein yet known: the Association also aims to improve agriculture and horticulture generally – organic methods especially; in its laboratory it analyses the nutriments of vegetables – important work to establish a survival diet; and, in order to lessen the inevitable 'preaching to the converted', it spreads its findings among other farmers and gardeners and in schools.*

One of the Association's projects has a special relevance to the impending food crisis and the vulnerability of city dwellers. It is 'Dig for Survival', a campaign backed by practical printed advice, using the combined wisdom of the 'Dig for Victory' campaigns of two world wars. Lawrence Hills reminds us that allotments of underpaid miners and the unemployed fed their families throughout the slump of the 1930s. Today he tells us: 'Four rows of carrots in a bed beside the path down the middle of the average semi-detached garden yield about 50 lb., replacing £4.50 worth of tinned at 9p a lb.. Four rows of potatoes replace about £16 worth of ready made deep frozen chips. . . .' To avoid fruitless competition, the Henry Doubleday Research Association has close

*Hills's major work is Comfrey: Fodder, Food & Remedy (Universe Books, 1976). His practical advice on organic methods appears in Fertility Without Fertilizers (Universe Books, 1977).

links with Britain's other major organic farming and gardening organisation, The Soil Association. This more formally constituted body, which has members in 56 countries and local groups throughout Britain, publishes a monthly magazine, runs courses, exhibits at agricultural and horticultural shows, and controls a company to market organically grown produce.*

These organisations may be said to represent the mainstream of alternative food production. Beyond that there lies another area where reputable people believe that growth and fertility are influenced not simply by the sun but by other, little-known forces. They acknowledge the ancient deference to planting by the moon and other phenomena; they seek to create a rapport between the grower and plants – the 'green fingers' touch – while some even avow the existence of 'plant spirits', whose communion must be enjoined if a garden is to flourish. In a world given to the worship of science, reason, and objectivity, such claims could be summarily dismissed if science and technology had delivered the promised Utopia, and if the crops and gardens of people, who might otherwise be dismissed as plain daft, were not living proof.

Elusive Magic

Peter Caddy had been in the Royal Air Force fifteen years before he and his wife Eileen had the experience which was to change not only their lives but those of many others. Resting on a journey near Glastonbury in the early 1950s, Eileen heard a voice which said clearly, 'Be still and know that I am God'. Although unprepared, she accepted it: from then on she was never without that 'still, small voice', and everything they did was with this guidance. A decade was to pass before they were guided to a place where they were to found a garden. The site was unpromising – a sandy caravan park in Findhorn Bay, on the Moray Firth, in the North of Scotland.

There, living with their three children and two friends in a cramped caravan, and almost penniless, they began to garden, enriching the sand with seaweed, rotting grass, stable manure –

*The basic ideas that led to the formation of the Soil Association and a detailed account of its fundamental research are contained in a book by its founder, Lady Eve Balfour, *The Living Soil and the Haughley Experiment* (Universe Books, 1976).

anything that came to hand. None of the group had gardened before, but in their first year they grew 65 different vegetables, 21 different fruits, and 42 kinds of herbs. As the garden took shape, one of their friends, Dorothy MacLean, found that she could receive messages from divine aspects of the plant world – the devas. For the garden to flourish, they were told, everyone working in it should radiate a sense of love and appreciation to the plants. The garden grew, and so did the community. The amazing began to happen: not only in the garden, which grew the now famous 42lb cabbage and the single broccoli plant which fed three families for several weeks, but in the community too. There, people sensed an enormous flow of energy – not *from* Peter Caddy, but *through* him; and those who came and stayed found this energy manifested in all their activities.

Today Findhorn is a community of 175, and anything up to 55 guests. The garden is still a focal point, but other activities include printing, weaving, macrame, pottery, and candlemaking, a shop, theatre, audio-visual, and building projects. These provide some income, but the rest 'happens'. When guidance is received to undertake a project, work begins, the money follows. In all Findhorn's twelve years of existence the means have never failed. Visitors to the community testify to the sense of energy, the cleanliness and generally high standards in everything attempted – yet without rigid rules, with no loss of spontaneity, and all the while with laughter and a feeling of joy. Now The Findhorn Foundation, University of Light, A Centre of Education and Research for Creative Living, the community sees itself as one of a number of centres of a New Age – a time for preparedness, when, despite man's destructiveness, the earth will come alive again.

Findhorn garden is not the Centre's only focal point, but it is still one that astounds many visitors. As Professor R. Lindsay Robb, a consultant to the Soil Association, wrote after seeing it: '. . . the vigour, health, and bloom of the plants in this garden at mid-winter on land which is almost barren powdery sand cannot be explained by the moderate dressings of compost, not indeed by the application of any known cultural methods of organic husbandry. There are other factors and these are vital ones!'

Magic Explained
Some 6,000 miles away I found a degree of the same inexplicable fertility in a garden on a bare, uncompromising hillside of clayey soil in coastal California. There I saw huge vegetables cheek by jowl with a riot of bright flowers and aromatic herbs. I spoke with Steve Kaffka, the bronzed, lithe young man running these student-powered gardens at the University of California – Santa Cruz – who went some way to explaining the inexplicable. 'Have you ever been in a garden where things seem to grow just well? Everything looks healthy, the way it should. You talk to the gardener and he tells you what he does; you go home and do the same, but your garden doesn't turn out the same way. You go back to him, but he can't explain why. In a lovely garden there's an atmosphere that helps everything to grow well. Healthy plants tend to have other healthy plants growing around them. Obviously, diseased plants spread disease; if they're covered with insects, the insects travel to other plants and attack them. A plant grown in good, fertile soil tends to be less attractive to insects than one grown in nutritionally deficient soil. Nature works to eliminate weakness, such as a weak plant – and appropriately so. So we think of a garden as a place which promotes well-being, and a gardener as a person who can try to create an environment for plants to grow. He doesn't *grow* plants – he just *helps* them – surrounds them with his care. There's nothing very mysterious about it. It involves knowing that nothing happens in nature that's not related to everything else. The caring gardener knows that some plants can influence each other and he tries to understand how. For example, there are root excretions which other plants can absorb; a kind of micro-life around the roots can have a carry-over effect on the roots of a different kind of plant; the substances produced in the soil by the type of micro-flora from one plant can have an effect on another kind – it may be

beneficial or it may not. The good gardener takes these subtle relationships into account.

'You could say that a carrot likes growing next to a carrot: it says, "Gee, there are other carrots here – it must be a good place for carrots, so I'll do well here." But proximity of like species is only good to the degree that it's balanced with other kinds of plant species. The association helps create a natural kind of environment – a mixture of shallow- and deep-rooting plants, seed producers and root producers, some plants attractive to certain insects and some attractive to others . . . vegetables, herbs and flowers. . . .'

He warned about the fashion for tidiness and uniformity. 'Insects are going to be in your garden. Accept them. One of the bad things about modern agriculture is that one cabbage has to look exactly like another: there mustn't be any little hole or blemish. The farmer has to resort to materials he'd rather not use, but he can't "make it" economically if he doesn't strive for this perfection, uniformity, and unnaturalness. It's something forced on him by the consumer – who in turn is led to expect it.'

I distinctly felt *naturalness* in the few acres of the hillside garden. No machine ever tore the soil or shattered the atmosphere of the place; the quiet was broken only by the sound of birds or voices – either those of students working, or that of Steve talking quietly to one of the many groups who come from far away to learn about the transformation.

Some distance to the north of Santa Cruz, at Palo Alto, I encountered John C. Jeavons of a lively group called Ecology Action of the Midpeninsular. There he told me how his precariously funded group had worked for the past two years to put figures to the horticultural methods used by Steve Kaffka to transform the bare Santa Cruz hillside into a flourishing garden. And what he told me was exciting. The initial research that the group had conducted on three-and-a-half acres seemed to indicate that the methods could produce an average of *four times* more vegetables to the acre than the amount grown by American farmers using conventional mechanised and chemical agricultural techniques. But that was not all. The methods also appeared to use *half* the normal quantities of water to achieve this four-fold increase, and – almost incredibly – once soil fertility had been raised, the energy needed was only a *hundredth* of that of commercial agriculture for every pound of vegetable grown!

Since no machines were used – only human muscle power – I asked him if the methods were not reduced to mere academic interest by the unrealistically high costs they would incur: I knew something of the hourly rate of labour in the United States even among relatively low-paid horticultural workers. The answer I received was unexpected. When the group projected the results from their trial plots to larger areas it was found that their methods actually produced *more gross dollars per acre* than commercial agriculture! In a world already short of food and facing shortages of energy to make chemical fertilisers, machinery, and indeed the fuel to run it, the methods – if widely applicable – could have revolutionary implications.

John explained to me that the methods were a marriage of two forms of horticulture begun in Europe around the turn of the century. In the 1890s, the fortunate gardeners around Paris were growing fantastic vegetable crops in 18 inches of the embarrassingly plentiful horse manure of the pre-motor age. This was unremarkable, but what was significant was the gardeners' discovery that, by growing vegetables so close together that their leaves touched, they created a mini-climate and a living mulch which choked weeds and held soil moisture. With the advent of the car, the gardens and their discovery were forgotten.

Some thirty years later, Rudolf Steiner, the Austrian philosopher and educator, pioneered a movement away from the recently introduced chemical fertilisers to gentler, balanced diets of organic ones as a cure for the growing incidences of crop diseases and pests. This he coupled with other ideas: companion planting; the growing of crops in raised beds, where a looser soil would allow air, moisture, warmth, nutriments, as well as the plant roots themselves, to penetrate the soil more readily; and sowing at certain phases of the moon.

Later an Englishman, Alan Chadwick, who had studied under Rudolf Steiner, combined the two methods. With them he transformed the Santa Cruz hillside which eventually passed to Steve Kaffka's care. The combination became known as the Biodynamic/French Intensive method.

Much more research still has to be done. Even if the preliminary astonishing results prove applicable to other climates and soil types, and to a wider variety of vegetables than those tested, limitations can still be expected.

Many organic vegetable gardens produce intensively only because their energetic gardeners cart in huge quantities of heavy organic manure – *their* alternative to convenient, relatively lightweight chemical fertilisers. Sometimes the loads are seaweed – but not everyone farms near seaweed; sometimes it is manure – pig, calf, or chicken from handy factory farms, from the stables of ornamental horses, or from town and city sewage farms. To assume that this input is available everywhere would be cheating: in the Third World, where most usable things are used, the quantity of waste is a tiny fraction of that available in affluent societies. Far more research is needed to determine true organic farming output – whether Biodynamic/French or any other method. In all probability it will be found that an uncomfortably high proportion of land must be regularly taken out of direct food production in order to grow crops specially for green manure or compost. If so, many optimistic claims will have to be modified.

Apart from this, nothing short of a revolution in land tenure, in social values, in a massive switch from eating meat and cereals to eating vegetables, or the rapid exhaustion of fuel sources would be likely to accomplish a switch from machine ploughing or rotovating to the laborious hand digging, composting, weeding, and hand watering which the Biodynamic/French Intensive method of horticulture demands.

Nevertheless, because of their faith in the work they are doing,

John C. Jeavons, Steve Kaffka, and their fellow workers well qualify to be termed survivalists. One day, mankind may be grateful for them.

The New Alchemists

California has been the fertile seedbed for a rich crop of alternative thinking destined to blow across the world and take root in one country after another. Throughout the 1960s a small group of scientists, artists, and humanists in America gathered together. What worried them most was a conviction that modern science and technology had spread a false confidence in techniques and abilities to solve problems. They were also disturbed that the new, respected tool of futurology was jeopardising man's survival through its ignorance of biology. To counter this they sought to protect social and biological diversity, and if possible extend them. In 1969 they formally organised The New Alchemy Institute – 'To restore the lands, protect the seas, and inform the Earth's stewards'.

Foremost among the Institute's founders were Richard Merrill, the Californian ecologist with a commitment to radical agriculture, and John Todd, a Canadian with degrees in tropical medicine, parasitology, and oceonography, and a doctorate in psychology and ethology. Activities began in Southern California, but before long John Todd and some of the group moved to Cape Cod on the East Coast, and there – almost accidentally – they acquired the lease of an 11-acre farm which became the Institute's first operational centre, coordinating projected activities in California, Costa Rica, and the Maritime provinces of Canada.

By 1972, the Institute's first projects were under way and its aims were clarified. 'We seek,' the group stated, 'solutions that can be used by individuals or small groups who are trying to create a greener, kinder world. . . . Among our major tasks is the creation of ecologically derived forms of energy, agriculture, aquaculture, housing, and landscapes, that will permit a revitalisation and re-population of the countryside.' The Institute hoped that it could initiate research projects in different regions which would reveal each one's special needs. With this in mind, the first centre at Woods Hole began studies intended to shape the skills which would be needed to establish modern, relatively self-contained communities, capturing their own power, growing their own foods and utilising their own wastes.

I had heard about The New Alchemy Institute before setting off for America, and Wood's Hole was one of my first ports of call. Unexpectedly I found myself in the heart of middle-class suburbia: all the trim houses facing the road, wide 'nature strips' and cars neatly parked on asphalt driveways. Then I came upon a remnant of countryside, a farm, and tell-tale windmills. I had arrived after all.

John Todd welcomed me warmly, and soon he was showing me round. The scene at once struck me as incongruous. Here was a farm – no ordinary farm, with its solar panels, windmills, fish tanks, greenhouse-domes, compost heaps and experimental plots – but a farm none the less. And here were John Todd and his friends experimenting in survival techniques and enjoying it to the full, while just over the treeline, middle-class Americans were intent on the serious business of suburban reality – cars, swimming pools, barbecues, martinis, dogs, hair-dos and shopping trips. But under the influence of John's knowledge, energy, and enthusiasm, and infected with the easygoing *rapport* of everyone on the farm, I quickly found myself totally absorbed in the people and their experiments.

First I learned about the Science for People programme. 'Rather than try and restructure the science establishment to become humanitarian, we thought it might be easier to make scientists out of humanitarians,' John explained. From this developed the idea of a network of collaborators, organic gardeners, and farmers around the country who would work with the Institute on experiments which seemed relevant to the needs of small groups.

Three research programmes involving them were in full swing, and one of these, the Backyard Fishfarm Project, was a focus of activity. Directed by Dr William O. McLarney – Bill to his friends

– it aimed to produce nutritious, good-tasting protein at zero cost, and, to do so, task number one had been to find fish which ate the algae at the bottom of the food chain – fish which would grow in such a way that a small group of people could provide all their own meat protein needs. The fish which most nearly filled the bill proved to be the highly productive African Tilapia, its only major drawback being the high-temperature water it needed to breed and grow – ideally 85 degrees Fahrenheit. Two trials were under way in pools covered with low-cost geodesic domes and plastic frames which effectively heated the water with the amply available solar energy. To speed growth, the Tilapia algae diet was supplemented with vegetable waste and insect life. A novel way to provide the insect life supplement at zero cost had been developed: in summer the district is plagued with midges or gnats, and it was found that light traps would catch at least an ounce of midges a day; a burlap curtain hung in manure-rich water soon became covered with midge larva, and to feed the fish they merely had to lay the curtains on the pond surface. Ponds were stocked from 1 May until 1 November; after then the Cape Cod winter prevented the water reaching the necessary temperature.

A second experiment was to search for food crops which possess a genetic ability to withstand insect pests and so grow healthily without constant applications of pesticides. As many organic growers have found on both sides of the Atlantic, too many over-enthusiastic claims are bandied about, and certain crops fall victim to certain pests even though every rule in the book may be matched with ample doses of Tender Loving Care. If chemical-happy commercial growers were to be converted to organic methods, someone had to identify the crops most suited to ecological management. This seemed an ideal project for collaborating organic growers – the kind of people most interested in finding the answer.

A third experiment was one initiated by Richard Merrill, to stimulate natural resistance to pests. Some plants give off chemical substances which repel certain insects, so a specific crop is interplanted with a second crop of a different species, by its nature repellent to any pest which may affect the first crop. Hundreds of collaborators across the country have worked on this experiment in companion planting, and their involvement has prevented the Institute from falling into the trap of assuming that what may work in Cape Cod will work everywhere.

The farm I walked over was the scene of many activities, all of them the subject of intensive record-keeping. One member supervised three wind-energy programmes. Another member was keeping rabbits over wire netting under which worms bred prolifically among the droppings – worms to feed fish or hens. Elsewhere a system for drying crops by solar heat was being tested. And everywhere experimental plots of vegetables and other crops were not only providing potentially valuable information but also feeding the ten full-time members of the community and their children, as well as part-time members when possible. Disseminating the new knowledge is seen as a vital part of the operation, so Nancy Todd, John's equally energetic wife, was running the publications division, not only publishing a regular journal but also books and pamphlets on experiments and findings.

'Activities' were only part of the picture, I soon learned, however. Because the suburban setting prevented the full-time members from living communally, they rented houses around. Far from lessening their sense of community, they found it allowed each family to live its own lifestyle, while coming together for work.

Lack of a permanent site, coupled with lack of funds, were the Institute's major problem. Each member was paid according to his needs – chiefly determined by the number of dependants, and modified by the kind of work done and the amount of outside income – spare-time writing, part-time employment and private means. By growing their own food, using scrap materials and maximum ingenuity on all projects, members kept outgoings as low as possible. For funds the Institute actively sought contributions from private sources and research grants, and canvassed for associate members.

The Message of the Tree
To talk to John quietly and without interruption among the
activities of the farm proved impossible, yet I wanted to learn
more about his own ideas. I suggested we find somewhere quiet,
and he took me to the edge of a lake where we sat undisturbed
among the trees.

There we talked about the need for change and how it might be
achieved. He told me of the chief events in his own life which had
led him to where he was. 'Around 1968 I was involved with a
network of other people studying the direct effects of man's
activities on the environment. We were looking at different
forms of stress behaviour in aquatic animals. I had previously
discovered hitherto unknown levels of social organisation in
fishes – cooperation and things like that – which were normally
considered exclusive to mammals and birds. We found that very,
very low levels of stress, whether DDT, oil, or thermal effects,
were capable of having an impact on aquatic animals: the disruption of key social signals, such as parent-young bonds, could
be jammed; they could be so easily interfered with. What we
could see was the unknown depth of whole populations or species;
and what made the equation even more dramatic was that those
animals with the highest forms of behaviour were most
susceptible to man's depredation. We began to see insidious
effects everywhere – and we weren't even beginning to study
the synergistic effects of two or three different kinds of stress.
Yet we knew that in the real world there were hundreds of
different kinds of stress affecting the system.

'So it induced a kind of doomsday panic in us and it became
clear that we had to *do* something. We also felt very guilty
about the whole business of just being doomsday chroniclers –
which is where most of the establishment research money
is going – rather than finding possibilities for restorative
approaches.'

I learned that this was perhaps the turning-point which led in
time to the creation of The New Alchemy Institute. He told me

of his hopes for its future – and some of his fears, especially the risk to the Institute and other alternative groups of over-exposure through the mass media, and the danger of being a 'seven-day wonder'. He stressed how he avoided the publicity which could swamp and destroy the Institute – and its ideas. 'Ideas don't spread that way; they grow through tight commitment – as did the Irish Monastic Movement in the fourth to sixth centuries. Those people had so much that was exciting to say that others were drawn to them like a magnet. I think the idea of living ecologically, which has fantastically spiritual and practical implications, requires almost the kind of involvement we normally associate with religion. When you begin to work with nature, you realise the *unknowingness* of nature. Your style changes. You feel so good about it that you tend to proselytise.'

It was then that John Todd told me of the tree near where we sat – the tree which spoke to him. 'It matters not whether it was my unconscious bringing to the conscious level some deeply-felt idea, but I was walking along at dusk. It was a disturbing period in my life – I was trying to level out the whole focus. I looked up and saw a tree – it must have been a nut tree, it had male catkins and they were hanging down. I'm telling this in the form of a story. I'm not trying to imply that the tree was *talking*, but it said: "You don't know me." I looked at the nature of the leaves and I *did* know the tree – it was part of my childhood, but something I'd known even as a child I'd forgotten: *its name*. And then it said: "You don't even know this place where you are; you can't tell me about the plants, the animals and what they mean . . . the *whole*." And then it said: "Without a sense of place and a sense of knowing, any claim to expertise is a hollow, cruel fallacy." It was a very humbling experience. I've condensed it greatly, but the essence of it was that to know a place was the beginning and there is no expertise in modern times – there are no experts. The experience was a mockery upon me. It began with, "You don't know me and yet I am part of your life," and then it went from there to, "You don't know the world around you and it is part of your life." And from there to the lesson, which was, "That's where one has to begin."

The Chinese Connection

Between the minority of survivalists in rich countries, unhooking themselves however painfully from the conditioning of the imposed consumer society, and the millions in the Third World, unsure of their ability to survive each day, there exist distinct, if tenuous, links. Most of the 'rich' survivalists have tried the imposed society, seen through its conditioning, and found it lacking. Most of the poor still believe the propaganda of élitists – their own and foreigners – that economic aid and growth will 'filter down' and save them while there is still time. This is one of the chief differences, though others abound. Nevertheless, many of them share the same sense of working with nature and the same abhorrence of violent, wasteful practices – few people more than the Chinese.

With a history of poverty and oppression, the Chinese people have not yet embraced waste as a way of life in the manner of the industrialised West. Before 1949 non-waste was a necessity; since then it has been elevated to a virtue, and in both agriculture and industry they are constantly exhorted to 'convert all waste to treasure'. Amid values where *use* replaces profit and ample labour can be mobilised to reclaim and recycle, beautiful things can happen. And, as one observer after another reports, they do: not by the 'cosmetic' bottle-collecting, pollution-controlling environmental approach of the West, but a basic, revolutionary approach to the way in which to live and treat the environment which supports them. Such a transformation could not have been achieved without the reform of land tenure which returned to people the responsibility of caring for their environment.

In the industrial West, human waste has become a taboo, to be flushed out of sight regardless of the consequences. The Chinese have no such hang-ups: they collect human waste in every way possible. Farmers build roadside privies to lure passers-by; in the cities the people place their soiled toilet paper in boxes to be burnt, so that the ash can be used as fertiliser; sewage plants treat the output from flush toilets so that all its potential fertility is returned to the land; bucket latrines are emptied into concrete tanks; boats heavily laden with city excreta ply the canals; strict precautions control tapeworm infestation and fly-borne disease: *all* water is boiled before drinking.

Everyone knows that the land must be nourished, and so, with the exception of rice straw, which is used as fuel for cooking, anything that could be composted is collected assiduously: vegetable waste, leaves and animal manure. Hessian bags are placed under oxen, horses and donkeys. Children collect city waste and sell it for pocket money. Green crops are ploughed in; weeds and silt are dredged from ponds and rivers; duckweed – elsewhere regarded as a curse – is cultivated on waterways for compost material, a central clearway being left for navigation.

The Chinese are taking some steps to avoid the mistake of reducing genetic diversity by developing varieties of grains and fruits to suit different regions. Water hyacinth, a pest in other countries, is grown as food for pigs and water buffalo.

Almost every kind of food is grown within their borders without imports of fertiliser or fuel, but it is in fish farming (aquaculture) that they excel. Before liberation many ponds were owned and operated by fish lords, but with the growth of the Commune movement the people turned their muscle power to deepening them, using the rich silt as fertiliser, and often more than doubling fish production. Now they enrich the ponds with pig manure, silk worm pupae, snails, sweet potato leaves . . . anything suitable that comes to hand – and every time they dredge them they carry more rich silt on to the fields. An impressive blend of work and ingenuity has created a self-perpetuating ecosystem.

When China and the USSR fell out, the Russians withdrew their technicians overnight, and the country ever since has had to rely largely on muscle power, on ancient skills, on recycling, and small, non-violent methods. In consequence 'soft' technology has survived more from necessity than virtue. Only recently have the advances of large-scale industrialisation and the vanguard of the consumerism society penetrated the body of her culture. At present the small and traditional exist alongside the large and technological in precarious balance. Harold Dickinson reports that poisons such as DDT and Benzene hexachloride have been widely used to boost food production and that now there is concern in some Communes about their cumulative effects to people and livestock. During his visit he frequently heard communards mention the need to find specific biological pest controls, but only once did he come across the practice.

The Chinese leaders are in the fortunate position of being able to exercise choice: whether to continue their policy of recentralisation, recycling, and limiting personal consumption, 'soft' technology co-existing with small-scale industry and such large-scale operations as may be necessary; or whether to pursue the same environmentally destructive policies as the USSR and the West. For students of survival – and the term may eventually embrace *all* mankind – China is almost certainly the most interesting country of all.

Chapter Eight:
Sharing and caring

Each survivalist must choose his own path, and, although the paths may be different, they do not necessarily lead to different places. If the one aim is to 'recentralise', as Peter van Dresser expressed it, those survivalists whose vision encompassed a whole region are not necessarily in conflict with genuine seekers of personal self-sufficiency. They are simply at opposite ends of a dazzling spectrum of experiment. Between them are a wide variety of groups: couples and families sharing homes and land; extended families; communities and communes, large and small.

Back in Britain from America I knew that I must talk with Robin Clarke and his communards of BRAD at Eithin y Gaer, for it was clear that they embodied so many of the principles I had encountered. I wanted to learn more of how they truly saw themselves: an escapist élite or a catalyst whose presence could help revivify the countryside, not only in their own Montgomeryshire, but as a model for other regions – in Britain, in other industrial countries, or in the Third World.

At BRAD, as in other communes, it is not easy to pin people down: so much is going on, and so little time is spent alone. But one evening I am with Robin Clarke in the farm kitchen and the moment is right for talking. I ask him how closely the commune which has evolved resembles what he had envisaged.

'When I had this idea of a rural community, one of the things I wanted to get away from was a world where certain highly specialised individuals planned our future . . . of the globe and all its 110 countries . . . a programme for this and that in which everyone's needs seemed to get perfectly ordered and ordained, so that they would be consuming x number of cucumbers per year and x number of kilowatts per year coming from x number of nuclear reactors and so on.

'When we started here, one impetus was to change the technology first – in other words get into soft technologies like sun and wind and methane and all these things. Behind a number of minds was the idea of a future in which everyone had a windmill and a solar roof and a methane digester and an acre or two of land between so many people. I now think that's just an alternative technocratic view: the only variable you change is the nature of the technology. That's where General Motors could well get in: as they stop manufacturing nuclear reactors and start making methane digesters and solar roofs, the future looks almost the same. You may have lessened the impact on *the environment*, but you haven't really lessened the impact on *people*; nor have you achieved any diversity or decentralisation.

'Two years ago I was much more enchanted with a global world view in which we would all switch to softer technologies – a kind of soft Utopia in which we would all live. The fundamental change in me is that I don't really believe in that any more. I don't think we should be working towards a situation where one does try to order all these things. You'd get the same problems as with technocracy itself. You'd get the missionaries, the zealots, the eco-freaks and all of them.

'I suppose my philosophy has become much more "the problem starts where you are" – that is, with you and your family, the people you live with. You sort out that situation and in the process you undoubtedly meet other people and you may be able to help them sort out their situation. And in some mysterious way, it's how I believe it should happen – starting from lots of different centres.

'One of the things I think is becoming more and more important is only distantly related to alternative technology, and that is the balance between population in the country and population in the towns and cities. It seems to me a very important thing we are doing here – it may prove to be the *most* important – and that's to be part of a movement to redress the balance.

'Montgomery is a county that's been disastrously under-populated for a long time. The only way the population loss is being checked is by bringing industry to the suburbs of the small towns that do exist, and I don't think this is the way to do it. The United Kingdom as a whole may or may not be overpopulated – I don't know. But I do know for sure that London is overpopulated and Montgomery is underpopulated. The inference is obvious: you have to find new ways of restocking the countryside. And that means more labour-intensive devices, larger groups living under one roof or under several roofs, and operating several small acres of land, and finding ways of doing it that make sense. And of course it's also good for the land. The more people you have on the land, the higher the productivity you should be able to get from it – without petroleum.'

I interject: 'But for this to happen you've got to offer people some stimulation. Small towns and villages are dull – not what city people are used to. We come back to the idea that a new set of values must either filter into society – or possibly explode.'

'Or people have to live through it and discover,' he adds. 'I don't think it's any good telling an eighteen-year-old that life in London palls after a while – I think he has to discover it. And maybe for him it *doesn't* pall. For lots of people it doesn't.'

'For some people, the idea of self-sufficiency has a tremendous attraction,' I remind him.

'I don't think the hermit solution is of any interest as a model, as a way of life, except for a few people,' he says with emphasis. 'This is where I have doubts about the rather puritanical insistence on self-sufficiency which the alternative technology movement has. After all, the idea is not to be self-sufficient, but to live in a community of people where there is trust and barter and under-standing . . . a coming and going, interchange and exchange. I think the move towards total self-sufficiency is a reaction against a total "unself-sufficiency" which one experiences in the industrialised world.'

I ask him: 'How can people with or without capital break out of the urban prison they're trapped in?'

'The only way the ones without capital can break out at the moment is the way some people here have done: by forming some kind of association with people who do have capital. We include the poor as well as the rich! But I've begun to doubt the whole ethic of "blueprintism" – the idea that whatever you do should somehow solve problems for others, whether a capstan lathe operator in Middleton or a Justice of the Peace working in the City. I think you just go barmy if you think in these terms all the time. I still think globally, mind you. When you're thinking about technology and alternatives to it, you have to. After all, there's no point in setting up a beautiful alternative technology system which exhausts all the copper reserves in the world. I don't mean that I want to hide my head in the clouds and ignore everything else except my own 40 acres – or whatever it happens to be. No, it's the blueprint thing that worries me.

'I think that the whole philosophy of what inspired the counter-culture, the communes movement, here and in the States, what inspired the freaks and the flower children and so many of the pop groups – the whole of that cultural change is not stamped by the philosophy of "blueprintism". The evolution of alternative technology, you see, comes from two sources: one was disenchanted technocrats like myself, where "blueprintism" was very much in evidence; the other was the counter-culture, where it wasn't. When they met there was a nasty period of friction while the devotees of the "hip" philosophy ran up against the devotees of alternative technocratism. What inspired alternative technology was the "hip" movement, not the disenchanted technocrats.

'When you go around communities, you find that a lot of them, at least unconsciously, revolt against any kind of blueprint ethic – any idea that *they* could be a model for anything else. They're just searching their own solutions, and if friends and neighbours find it useful, they pass it on.'

We gaze into the fire for a moment, and then I say: 'I've been asked, "Suppose you start an ecological community and in time get it all working smoothly, what will hold it together then?" '

He is quick to counter: 'Go to the top of the hill here and look down on these 40-odd acres and just begin to rehearse in your mind the things that we might do with it. I couldn't see them all being done within my lifetime: experiments in aquaculture, from algae to big carp, with all the labour involved and the research into how to feed them from the farm; and that should be coupled with making use of the farm's water power; and permanent pasture management isn't nearly as simple as you'd think – herbal leys for example; then there's a whole 10 acres of woodland of which only about three have any worthwhile timber, leaving seven to plant – the whole concept of woodland farming that's being brought into Africa, in which you siphon off some of the woodland's productivity by raising semi-domesticated animals which feed off it without harming it. There's much in favour of re-introducing woodland into the farming "menu", but it's not being done, which is one reason there's so little wood left and why the countryside looks so bloody bare. Work to do here? There's two or three years' work on building the second house over the hill as well. No, I can't see any end to it.'

My talk with Robin Clarke has helped me to understand the community as he sees and feels it, but I need to hear from others. Later, I ask three early members, John and Maria Clemow and Mike Ellsworth, if they will tell me how the experiment is working for them, and they agree readily.

John Clemow, I learn, first became interested in the idea of a utopian community when he was eighteen, but he had become the middle-aged managing director of a pharmaceutical company before he eventually decided to drop out. It was then that he met Robin Clarke, whose technological ideas seemed to complement his own sociological ones. John Clemow was accustomed to making important decisions incisively: he promptly resigned his post and made available to Robin much of the money the project needed to get off the ground.

When John tells me this, I am in his room, the only spot on the farm that he can call his own. We are sprawled on the bed with his American-born wife, Maria. The room is big enough for the bed, some bookshelves, and a chest of drawers . . . little more, and it is hard to reconcile these surroundings with the 'expense account' world of pharmaceuticals. I ask him how he felt at the time he made the decision.

'I felt good about it. It was a boyhood dream coming true. It wasn't a case of waking up one morning and saying, "My God, civilisation is crashing, I've got to get out"; more a feeling of excitement at finding that something I had in my mind was complemented by something in somebody else's mind. And the two made sense.'

'Now that it's happened, how well does reality match the dream?' I ask.

'I'm getting an enormous amount of physical satisfaction. The only physical exercise that was possible in urban business was completely divorced from normal life; but here you feel your mind and body as one entity rather than two separate things.'

I ask how they feel about being privileged people, able to buy their way out of the system, and John replies: 'When you look at the amount of capital per person we're spending it's not much. With ten in the community so far, we've spent £2,000 each. A young couple buying a home would have to find considerably more than £2,000 each. Sharing makes sense: put one washing machine between ten people instead of two and obviously there's a saving.'

Maria adds: 'We're also trying to use less of other manufactured goods, remember.'

I ask: 'How easy is it to do without?'

'If I don't see the goods, I just don't think about them, but as soon as I'm surrounded by consumer goods, I can feel myself getting sucked in. I resist, but I can feel the attraction . . . I walk down the high street and look at the clothes and I feel it would be nice to have this or that. . . .'

I ask her: 'I know a little of why John dropped out: what prompted you?'

'I've moved in straight society but I've never worked at anything I really wanted to do. I've always felt that anything I might decide to do would cut off – sort of – 80 per cent of myself, because I would have to do *one* thing. I felt I could evolve with just one person, but evolve much further with more people. Robin's soft technology idea completed the picture and offered a way of life in which I could be doing lots of *different* things which all seemed to be tied together as a whole. But the community experience would be totally invalid if it didn't go beyond just altering the *technical* aspect of things . . . if it left aside the essential role balance between the sexes. In straight society all that can happen is that maybe women can get a better chunk of things; what's needed is a complete transformation of the relations between the sexes.'

'Does it happen here?'

'It hasn't got very far yet. We've taken a step on the superficial level: everybody does the kitchen and there's an equality of tasks you couldn't find in straight society, but we should go way beyond having to think in these terms. What's too bad is that community living is more attractive to men. It continues to be a male-orientated, male-dominated thing. Women tend to have more problems in community life because they're examining things at a much deeper level.'

We talk on, and then I realise it is getting late and I leave. Back in the communal area only a few people are still around, talking quietly near the wood stove, and one of them is Mike Ellsworth. Despite the hour, he suggests we talk, and we settle down in his room.

Mike, I discover, left school without any academic qualifications and promptly applied himself to the serious business of earning a living as a timber merchant, leavened by an interest in theatre and drama. Life continued to be earnest and untroubled by questioning doubts until he married, and then a change began. He explains: 'Under the stimulus of my wife I had a growing interest in ideas, and my mind began to work a bit.' In fact, so interested in 'ideas' did he become that, at the age of thirty-seven and with a growing family, he sold the business he had built and went to technical college to take his 'A' levels. By now he could see a new career path, and he went on to Manchester University to read drama with the intention of teaching drama in education.

For a while it seemed that he had found his niche, but then, as he explains: 'A profusion of ideas came to me through contact with young people, and I began to understand what they were reacting against. I realised that the education system as it exists wasn't something I could believe in.'

For Mike this was indeed a time of change, for not only was he disillusioned with his plan, but his marriage was also under strain. One of the ideas he had encountered was the concept of living in community: now he felt that in a community situation the family might be held together.

'I happened to talk to someone in Liverpool who knew John Clemow. I wrote to him and got a very warm letter back. We came down here and met the people, and immediately I felt this was what I wanted.' The family moved into Eithin y Gaer, and Mike began to fulfil his ideas in group living, to work on the land and develop alternative technologies. Three months later he was still at Eithin y Gaer, but alone. 'You could say that I came here through an experiment,' he says pensively.

'What were you looking for here?' I ask.

'For me the technological is subservient to what happens between people. I believe that the only real revolution is a psychological one, and that it's *us* that have to change now . . . the way we apprehend each other, relate to each other. The economics of this place are sound. We can work towards self-sufficiency without a great deal of pain – a challenge I'm sure will be met. But what at the moment is the difficulty is a collective inability to throw away crutches – a fear on some people's part about the dangers of letting their defences down. Visitors can be a problem in this: they can be an excuse for postponing things between people. And it's group growth that one is interested in. If people can't learn to accept each other as unique individuals, rather than some sort of patterned social creature, I don't see much progress being encountered.

'There's a danger in joining a community with a set number of ideas about what it should be – the dangers of it becoming institutionalised are always there. One can become some sort of fiction for other people to write about, rather than try to live in harmony with each other, or accepting each other's hostilities as pretences; letting your feelings flow – that's what it really is. This is not happening. We're not getting angry. We're not kicking hell out of each other. We're more tight-lipped and polite instead of letting fly. I think that everybody who's come here has some form of alienation from the other society or from other people – out of crisis, I think.

'We've got to look at the local community – that's the most important thing for me – that one tries to spread one's ideas on a local scale first . . . make the farming community understand what we're trying to do. There's very little contact with them at the moment because we haven't really escaped the demands of building and getting the farm together. We're always postponing, saying there's no time to do this, no time to get an arts centre going or a choral group or a pottery group and so on.'

'So this frenetic activity,' I ask, 'is getting in the way of your getting together as a group and preventing you from integrating with the local community. . . . The people who can help outside. The local schoolmaster, the vicar, the parish elders if you like. Getting into rural politics.'

He reflects on that for a moment and then takes up the theme in a different way. 'I was in Bangor the other day. I was buying a book and it was pouring with rain, and I said to the girl in the shop: "I'm glad it's raining," and she couldn't understand it. I said: "Your food needs it – you've got to have some rain, otherwise it won't grow." But to her, food was just something you went into a shop and bought! She was totally alienated from the responsibility of feeding herself. That was something I was once alienated from too: shop windows were always full. But, the joy of knowing that whatever happens in world markets, provided God is kind, we can grow our own food here and survive. That seems to be the basic responsibility one has for one's life – to be able to grow one's own energy.'

'But you've bought your way out of straight society, and you still depend on it . . .'

'Perhaps, but at least we're demonstrating by what we're trying to do that resources can be put to more positive use than they are at the moment – the pursuit of material wealth and so on. The very fact that we're experimenting with our lives is to say that we no longer accept that there is only one form of so-called bureaucratic, centralised social democracy, so that people become aware, if only gradually, that there are other ways. And the pressure on resources will ultimately be reduced as more and more people adopt these ways of living.'

'Can you offer anything for the ordinary person, disenchanted with city life, but with no capital?'

'We've three people here who came without money – there's no question of their feeling inferior citizens. I think we've got to attract more people to come into the country so that we can have a more labour-intensive form of farming. We can't go on depending on other countries for all our food – or on decisions made in Brussels. If we can show that a group of people on 44 acres, farming organically with labour-intensive methods and trying to return to the old, more traditional kinds of pastures and leys, while working towards autonomy, can succeed, then we shall have demonstrated that work is available on the land which doesn't need a money economy in the way we understand it in order to support it.'

Three other people at BRAD interest me – Ruth and Roger Palmer and their small daughter Ellie – who are up here with a view to joining. While working with Roger, building a wall, I had learned that he had been twenty years in the Royal Navy, leaving as a

Chief Petty Officer, and that Ruth had been a nurse and social worker. They seem level-headed, reticent to air their views. I am intrigued. One evening we have a chance to be together, and I ask them why they are here. They tell me how, on paper, their careers have been exemplary – 'pillars of the establishment' they describe themselves – but I learn that, as the years went by, they found themselves increasingly alienated, so that in their private lives they became 'firm outsiders'. The change took a positive shape about five years ago.

'We had a group of friends,' Roger explains, 'lively, intelligent people whose thinking wasn't what is accepted as normal in society – they were anti-establishment. But we found – as we have with so many others since – that we were just sitting talking and nobody was going to get up and do anything. This was the point at which we decided that we *would* – and the first thing we did was to go to Australia. We'd heard it was the promised land and about the communes at Kuranda. We hiked up there to find the groups living there, and we found the sort of people who have made communes very much a word to be looked sideways at. We found bunches of kids up there living in the trees, all the girls were pregnant, all the guys were smashed out of their heads – it was pretty messy. They weren't doing anything constructive at all. Nobody knew what was going on; they were just living together as a group. It was a bitter disappointment because we'd understood that there were groups of people who *were* together, who'd gone to Australia because of the climate and the obvious advantages of being able to live out.

'So we came back from Australia with no set ideas except that we wanted to do something different. We didn't know what: we only knew that the conventional lifestyle wasn't what we wanted and we didn't feel we were making any contribution to life either.' Ruth had her nursing; Roger felt he wanted to work for the community and eventually joined a Home Office pilot scheme which offered offenders community service as an alternative to prison. But not for long: 'I resigned because I could see how it was being mishandled . . . being used as a punitive measure rather than rehabilitative,' he explains. From then on they both worked outside the establishment, converting derelict cottages, farm work, pottery, odd jobs; and Roger hitch-hiked from Shropshire to the Hebrides and back to look for a farm.

I ask whether they had retained the original idea of living communally, and Ruth answers: 'We've kicked the idea around, but this is the only time we've been close to doing it. Roger has been in favour of it for some time, but I've only considered it since I had a child.'

'What do you see as the advantages of it for a woman?'

'They're tremendous. Children have other children around. In a standard nuclear family they suffer from a heavyweight of parenting. Even after only a day here Ellie feels the weight off her – and I feel the weight off me. I haven't got to be watching every minute – there'll be someone around. That leaves both of us freer to develop. The lot of a woman trapped in the traditional suburban home by housework and children seems appalling. And it's so *easy* to have an alternative. Fifty years ago when urban and rural life was much more open, families weren't so isolated from each other; you knew everybody in the street if you lived in a town, all the families supported each other, and the kids played in each other's houses.'

I ask Roger what he found wrong with straight society.

'The apathy. The sheer inability of the great mass of people to comprehend that there's anything wrong: that we're going to run out of resources; that there's any need for an alternative; that people like us are a bunch of nuts, tinkering about with wind-mills. When I was in social service I could talk alternatives to people and I'd get completely blank looks – they thought it was either subversive or vaguely naughty. "Alternative to what? We're all right. What's wrong?" they asked.

'We had six months in Telford New Town and I was into every kind of community activity. But all the time I came up against the desolation of people who had nothing spiritual, nothing inside them. Soulless. Watching TV, reading newspapers, eating tinned beans. Letting their souls drift into a wasteland. . . . The number of offenders I met who were in trouble simply because life was too complex for them; and how few were the people who had the compassion to give any time to helping them. There's *always* been petty crime, but people used to have compassion and time to deal with it in a reasonable way. But if I suggested to anyone something was wrong, I met this blank look. I felt too lonely. When once in a while you meet someone who does understand, you just know instinctively.'

'I felt lonely too,' Ruth adds. 'I heard everything from Roger and I could only *reflect* what he said – I couldn't *contribute* anything. There wasn't anybody who was on the same wavelength at all.'

'Coming here,' Roger says, 'finding that everyone *is* – that's the most binding thing of all.'

Before I left Eithin y Gaer, I told Roger and Ruth of my own plans to convert an old cottage and revive six acres of countryside. Some weeks later, just before I moved from London, I received a letter from them. It said simply: 'Your wall stayed. So have we. We've joined BRAD on a permanent basis, and hope to grow with it. We stand ready to help you at any time.'

Few people who have spent any time at BRAD can be left in doubt about the seriousness of the project, nor fail to be impressed with the technical quality of what has been built. Neither is there doubt in the minds of its members about its aims to revive the countryside, develop alternative technologies, and work as a group – the whole serving as a model for a society with changed values. What does come across, however, is some difference of viewpoint about the order of importance. Some would like to see more emphasis on the personal growth of each member, some on creating a stronger community spirit. A visitor may be left with the feeling that the almost total immersion in activity – from planning and physical work to looking after visitors – serves as a safety valve for unresolved conflicts and a means of avoiding confrontation. In consequence feelings are repressed and those who think of the commune more as a place of retreat than a place with a mission are left unsatisfied.

On one point there can be no dispute. Everyone there is participating in an experiment which has never been tried before. Everyone there has been through university and, but for the decision to participate, might be riding on the familiar ineffectual merry-go-round from which George Willoughby and John Manson eventually alighted.

A few months after my visit I learned that Robin and Janine Clarke had left. Their plans were to farm on their own nearby. Along with others who knew him and BRAD, I was surprised at the news, yet looking back I could see the seeds of division which grew to bring about the final break. At the heart of the problem was the flow of visitors and the frenetic activity which the majority of the group felt was impairing the way its members were relating to each other. For Robin, however, visitors were essential to stimulate both the group and outside interest in alternative technology. His decision to leave reflected the group's determination to become a community first and a research centre second, although work on alternative technology continued unabated, if less publicly. Robin's departure shook them, but, thanks to the strong foundations he helped to build, it survived.

Royal Fillip

A short distance west of struggling Eithin y Gaer, deep in a derelict slate quarry, is a community of a very different kind. There, visitors are anything but a threat – they are essential to its aims, and provided they work they are welcome. Publicity is welcome too, for it hopefully attracts the flow of funds and materials from the Establishment that the place needs to make it tick. The community is the National Centre for Alternative Technology and Resource Conservation, located just outside the small town of Machynlleth. There, a nucleus of permanent communards, amply helped by transient volunteers, are converting the quarry into a near-self-sufficient AT research and demonstration unit appropriate to its impressive name.

I visited the community in its early days, when the Wagnerian grandeur of the massive cliffs and towering slate heaps was barely disturbed and the few grey buildings were still chiefly in ruins. Some eight months later, however, the site was to boast an impressive array of standard AT hardware: super-insulated houses (both traditional and imported), a methane digester, a solar panel, a small-scale hydro-electric generator and a windmill. The key to this swift transformation is its charismatic organiser, Gerard Morgan-Grenville – director of two companies far removed from the Alternative: one processing stainless steel and the other dealing in fancy glassware and china. However, his intimacy with the industrial scene enabled him not only to secure substantial gifts of fibre-glass, batteries, turbines, solar panels and other goodies from some sixty companies, but also to organise working volunteers from universities and elsewhere so quickly and in such numbers that within the eight months the Centre was able to hold a national press conference coincidentally with a visit from the Duke of Edinburgh, no less.

The Centre itself is an offspring from a charity, The Society for Environmental Improvement Ltd, which was set up in 1972 with a £50,000 grant from an anonymous backer. With Gerard as its chairman the society planned to become a link between big business and the environmental movement. Twenty years in industry and an involvement in marketing forecasts had made him acutely aware of the impending resource shortage; while the sensitive eye of an amateur artist had sharpened his concern over pollution. He soon became convinced that the crisis had already arrived. As he explained to an interviewer from *Undercurrents* just before the royal visit, 'I then thought, well, everyone who can do anything about this ought to try and do *something*. So I set about trying to get some funds, and as you know got some. Then we spent a whole year just looking at the whole environmental problem and trying to see what we could do that was not being done by anyone else and which could be done on the sort of money that we had, and the sort of skills which we might be able to obtain. Everything fell into place suddenly and this centre was born as an *idea*, and very shortly afterwards in practice as a project.'

To critics of his methods – hob-nobbing with royalty and capitalists – he is unrepentant: 'I think that people perhaps at the lower end of today's pyramid fail to appreciate that some of the people who control industry are in fact highly intelligent and fairly wise, fairly far-seeing individuals.' He complains that there is far too much talk and not enough doing, and he says of the majority of communes in Britain: '. . . they are unbelievably fragile, and they don't really add up to a saleable commodity in the latter part of the twentieth century. The ones that survive . . . tend to be the religious ones. I think a very important point to realise is that we've got an external interest here at the Centre, whereas most communities are internal – they're interested in their own survival, doing their own thing.' Although the Centre aims at self-sufficiency, it also exists to serve people outside, he is careful to point out. And he points to a crying need for more similar institutions which can demonstrate that people can get together and show how it is possible to have a better life. He describes the excitement of visitors to the Centre who find themselves working with the permanent communards on real, life-sized problems. Time and again they have been heard to say: 'Thank goodness we've found a place where it is happening.'

The Outriders

Into much of the thinking world there is at last filtering a recognition that conflict exists between the way the imposed society is developing and the environment's capacity to withstand it. In consequence, new hunting grounds have been opened up for sociologists and other scientists to observe, measure, predict, and publish. Much of their research has focused on how man has disrupted and degraded the environment; some of it has studied the way a few societies – especially primitive ones – manage to live in harmony with nature; and at the same time ideas have been aired on how hypothetical societies of the future might use accumulated knowledge to maintain – in place of conflict – a balanced interaction between man and nature.

In one university at least, those involved in such research have felt constrained to go further than theorise: they have wanted to join the ranks of the survivalists and actually do something. This has happened at the University of Lancaster, where, in the Programme of Peace and Conflict within the Department of Politics, Hugh Miall and Joseph Valadez not only initiated plans to found a community of up to 800 people, but travelled across the world to a promising almost unpopulated area in a search for the ideal site. They had to find a place where man had made little or no impact on the environment, for, as the initiators put it: the experiment was intended to throw light on the ways in which man's activities affect the environment, how these effects could be ameliorated, and what problems arose when changing from ecologically 'imbalanced' to 'balanced' forms of social organisation. To gauge the community's impact they planned to study the ecosystem 'before and after', to test a number of proposed conservation measures, and to observe what happens to the people involved and to their technologies in the transition process.

Although the way that volunteers for the community would be chosen was not worked out in detail, they would be drawn mainly from industrial societies – though, to keep its international scope, not from any single culture or country. Age and sex distribution would help stabilise the population; a range of skills would be sought, as well as diversity in cultural outlook and world view. The pioneers were expected to emerge from those who worked on the early stages: the community was expected to be established within two or three years.

At the University an interdisciplinary team set about co-ordinating the design of the community with specialists in other fields. Agriculture would be 'organic', technologies 'intermediate', and energy recycling systems would be developed. The initiators wanted the human community to become part of the 'information flow' of the natural system. They had no desire to manage or regulate it; they simply wanted to live in a way that would allow the whole – human and natural – to become 'a self-organising system in dynamic equilibrium'.

The team went a long way to anticipating the working of the community itself – its decision-making, leadership, information flow, conflict resolving, division of labour, rewards and territory allocation. The project was discussed at the 1972 UN Conference on the Human Environment in Stockholm, and attracted sympathetic interest from a number of leading scientists and institutions. The choice of site was clearly paramount. It should be uninhabited – or nearly so – yet large enough and fertile enough to support the community, pollution-free, far from cities and industrial centres. The ecosystem should be closed and definable, and minimally degraded. Moreover, the host country and its university should be willing to cooperate and help to sponsor the project. After much study, one location emerged as having all the necessary criteria, and it was to this area that Hugh Miall and Joseph Valadez travelled for a strenuous February and March in 1973 – to Aysen in southern Chile, where they found almost all they had hoped for.

In September, when agreement was well under way in Chile, the military tyranny seized power, dismissed university rectors and suspended research projects.

Undaunted, the project's initiators hope that the situation may be temporary. 'It would be a mistake,' they say, 'to abandon a long-term project, which we feel could benefit Chileans and hopefully the world, on account of what may be a short-term political development.' Nevertheless they have begun to consider alternative sites, and if Chile is out, the project will happen somewhere else. To progress work and draw in others, a conference/ workshop was held near the University in July 1974.

The initiators do not see their community project merely as a 'one off' effort, but as a precursor to many others, forming – in association with other communities already in being – a network of communities throughout the world. The communities will develop contacts, they say, not only with the indigenous people around them, but with other communities in different ecosystems to exchange survival information. The initiators see this network not as a federation, but as a self-organising system and a counter to the anticipated move by collapsing western industrial societies towards global control of the biosphere. 'This begins with global monitoring,' they warn, 'but cannot stop before it reaches the idea of global ecological management.' The initiators see this as bad ecology because it threatens to centralise still further man's place in the biosphere. 'It will require an extension of man's interference in ecosystems not merely to exploit them but bring them under control,' they say. Such centralisation will threaten to deplete genetic variety still further – but that is not all: ecological control will only be possible if *social* processes are also controlled.

The proposed network represents an alternative means of global ecology: communities will adapt to their own environments, but at the same time they will interact so that they have an organisation as a whole. In this way they will also develop an ability to adapt to any variations in the global environment which affect them all – a promising form of alternative organisation, the initiators believe, for a biosphere they see as being in a state of 'dynamic disequilibrium'.

For Those Who Cherish Wilderness
In Canada two doctors – husband and wife – have sunk most of their resources into plans for a community near Vancouver. The site, a place of wilderness, once settled but now empty, is on an island: 410 acres at the end of an eight-mile mountain trail and bordering the sea. They describe its great variety of environments: '. . . from rain forest type to tropical arbutus groves, with lovely open views and dark cool corners. There are all types of trees, a magical all-year-round sweet water creek, and meadows and old fruit trees . . . a few old barns which can be restored.'

The sponsors, Robert Makaroff and Shauna Little, say that their first priority is the area's wilderness; their second is 'the development of physical systems which allow humans to live in a nondestructive balance with their environment'; and their third they describe as 'social justice . . . as we see it in this time and place in history, namely equality on the physical level, such as food and housing'. The land will be open to the public as a wilderness reserve for camping and hiking, but closed to cars. Permanent and semi-permanent residents will supervise its use, clear up the mess left by past logging, and build camping sites and shelters – all compactly clustered. The site will not be just a place for people who want to build a house. Residents will also carry out experiments in alternative energy and pollution control. Campers and hikers who bring their own food and tent will pay nothing nor be expected to work; but those who use the shelters for any length of time will be expected to contribute by working, putting in money and by barter.

All of this is vastly different from their original plan which envisaged a quick build-up to a community of around 600 and a rapid transition to complete democratic self-government, the sponsors phasing out their initial control until they had equality with others. Difficulties over purchasing enough land and delays with bureaucrats forced them to delay their programme, but Robert Makaroff sees this as: 'A breathing spell which in retrospect has been a piece of very good fortune, because our thinking has changed quite significantly. If we had begun to try to do some of the things we had planned a year or two ago, the project would most certainly have come to an untimely end. The major shift in our thinking has to do with control, and we now see very little prospect of our project becoming "democratic" in the way that most young people understand the concept. Shauna and I will be making the decisions, hopefully as Directors of a private, non-profit Trust, when the land is turned over to the Government – as it will be. This will happen as soon as possible so as to induce the Government to buy adjacent land as a green belt reserve. Our project will be a "company" town, to be blunt, or a "theocracy" like the Hutterites. The transition has been a painful one, at least for me. It's not pleasant to be regarded by daily associates as an oppressive "power-tripper" and neo-fascist. I have come to believe that people seeking alternative or intentional communities must face this issue (of control) more openly and more honestly than they do now, if they hope to make the experiment more than a very transitory one – valuable as that sort of experience may well be for them. And so now our lowest priority is transition to a pure democratic socialism. We suspect that this is unattainable at this time, and probably not within our lifetime – possibly not at all. In no way will preoccupation over this sad realisation be allowed any longer to interfere with the three new priorities.'

His dream is still that such a group might reach the size which originally seemed desirable, but he would halt it at any level which seemed to threaten the land or the social organism.

To understand the change in control, it is necessary to appreciate his world view. 'Humans, as a species, have swarmed. The planet's environment has been drastically altered, and mostly for the worse, so that a vicious cycle is accelerating. Only disciplined control can change that situation in a humane way. To the degree that democracy exists at all, it is totally incapable of doing so at this late stage. In the developed world it only augments the problems, making it impossible to envisage interruption of consumerist appetites . . . true social justice is denied by an élite which rules by the use of distractions, the manipulation of mythologies: in short, the carrot instead of the stick. In the less wealthy countries, mass pressures exert an increasing, mindless pressure, and the élite enforces some sort of order and harsher social injustice with the use of the big stick.'

He sees two future scenarios. In one, present conditions continue until human populations are cut back – probably in horrible ways – with the survivors living longer into 'the twilight of the planet's cosmic senescence than might have been the case if no drastic crises had occurred'. In the other, such crises are avoided, populations reach 12 billion within a few hundred years and 'the poor old planet will not last long with such a load of human protoplasm'.

He admits: 'The temptation to abandon all altruistic effort and "live it up" in the here-and-now will be much stronger. As age, flagging energy and horror at the events around us press upon us, the urge to swim against the current weakens. Yet the urge to transcend personal comfort remains to nag us . . . to know if we *can* be content with less, to know how *much* less, to know if human resourcefulness *can* find answers to basic needs which can be balanced against the earth's resources. To die, knowing there *could* have been humane solutions to the problems our species faces – even though there is almost no chance of adopting them – seems better than dying in utter despair.'

Success on a Slender Thread

The history of communes and communities is strewn with failures. Not many have lived more than a few years, and yet this in itself is no condemnation of the movement, for, as each dies, another comes into being: it is a *continuing* movement, a constant searching towards Utopia – whether the broad vision of the Lancastrian project, or a haven where a small group can feel free from the oppressions of the world outside.

During my journey I encountered communities which were flourishing and floundering; and I met people who had been members of ones which had failed. I learned that a community had a far greater chance of success if all its members were clear about what it was trying to do. While at a community I would speak separately with members and find that each had a different concept of what the community was all about – in effect each was in a different community! Not only should the group's aims be clear, but each member should have a strong commitment to them. He should have a sense of having renounced his old way of life and embraced the new one, and, if the act has involved some real sacrifice, the transition is beneficially more marked. Ideally the member should have made some kind of investment in the community – not necessarily money, it could be skills, talent or physical work given to a group over time without expectation of reward.

Much depends on how the community is run. To achieve its aims, the members must plan ahead, remembering that a plan need not be final – it can be changed at any time. On many sad-dening occasions I learned of precious time, energy, and funds wasted in misdirected effort – either from not having any plan, or through disregarding lessons which could have been learned from other groups, from 'straight society experts', or from history. When energy was also dissipated in overcoming the stresses of living closely with others during a time of building, learning new skills, coping with the unexpected almost every day, communities foundered – or came perilously close to doing so.

There must be a fair way to reach decisions. Most groups I met did so by consensus, accepting the extra time expended as an investment in getting to know each other and their aims. In some communities there may be a permanent leader; in most, only a leader for the duration of each specific project. The choice seems to depend on the aims of the group and its collective conscious-ness. Some way of resolving conflicts is essential: frankness coupled with a sense of timing and an appreciation of the other's state of mind would seem to be prime ingredients. Many conflicts can be avoided if the group has a good *rapport*, so that potentially conflicting situations don't arise. Again, conflicts can be reduced if everyone knows who is supposed to be doing what: too much permissiveness erodes the vital sense of commitment, breaks up the group, obscures its aims and gets in the way of efficient run-ning of the place. *Rapport* is helped if the group meets frequently – some prefer regular meetings at fixed times, others as the need arises or when the 'vibes' are good.

To live in a community it is a help to *like* people: if any person's feeling of alienation is temporary – perhaps the result of over-involvement with the imposed society – and the group has therapeutic leanings, this obstacle need not be insurmountable; but everyone has to be willing to exercise more tolerance than the world outside normally shows. Since work *must* be done – and only the members can do it – there is no room for the persistent shirker. However, the group must recognise that an 'awkward' member may be doing his best, and with support of caring people will eventually make some kind of contribution: he may inspire with songs and humour, come up with bright ideas, heal rifts, who knows what? Once 'efficiency' is no longer expressed in money terms, contributions become valid in unexpected ways. The most effective way to discipline the occasional or persistent deviant is group censure: if he loses the love and respect of the group he will either conform or leave.

Not surprisingly, when joining a group, people tend to show their best side and hide their worst – often the group they seek to join behaves similarly. Two 'rules' can help at this stage: any newcomer should undergo a lengthy probation period during which he or the group can dismiss each other with no recriminations; early in this period each must reveal, however painful the experience, any known serious faults, neuroses, weaknesses, deviations, and idiosyncracies. In the closeness of the group situation these are sure to be revealed in time: it is infinitely less hurtful all round if the revelation happens early.

A community is only a community if there is some boundary between it and the world beyond. The boundary need not necessarily be territorial – marked by a high wall, portcullis and drawbridge – it may be the difference in values, living standards, attitudes, religion, political view . . . but the stronger the boundary, the stronger the community – and herein lies one of the chief dilemmas of the community ideal. If the group is to be more than a retreat – if it is to be a model of Utopia or an alternative society – then it cannot make its point in complete isolation: its ideas will not spread. On the other hand if any caller at the gate can enter, if visitors may come and go at will, if members may leave and return as they wish, boundaries fade and all the essential bonds of renunciation, sacrifice, commitment, and communion are weakened.

Alternative under Fire

The complex area of boundaries, with its nuances of élitism, parasitism, and escapism, attracts some of the strongest criticism of the commune and intentional community movement – and not only from those committed to the imposed society. Harold

Dickinson, staunch supporter of so many of the survivalists' ideals, is one such critic – not so much of the integrity of the members' motives as the relevance of their experiments to what he sees as *real* problems rather than those rooted in self-indulgence.

Late one night on the outskirts of Salzburg, when the moment was right, he told me of his doubts of the alternative society and intentional communities. 'They've got to be a model,' he stressed. 'They've got to show that in the long run they can be self-sufficient to the extent of surviving without the back-up of advanced, high-technology society. Many of them are using materials and devices and artifacts which are dependent on the productive capacity of the society which they have left. Yet their members still go back to health services and social security, still accept their pension rights, while believing that they are having nothing to do with the illness of the society they have left. By avoiding them they are failing in their political and social duty. If they believe they have such a duty, by all means let them conduct the experiment, but at the same time let them use their actions as a basis for influencing society. Just to hive themselves off and say "Look, we're doing no ecological damage because we've set ourselves up in this way" is not an example to anybody. Instead of staying in the filthy harbour, they've moved out to sea in their splendid yachts, and so they don't see what it's like in the shambles of the seafront any more. To be any good, they must stand up to examination in detail and emerge as pretty close to self-sustaining examples that others can follow. Otherwise they're just an opting out – they're not an alternative society at all.'

I broke in: 'But surely the answer is to use *some* of the outputs of straight society, but not others – to *discriminate* and use those which are concerned with *needs* and survival rather than *wants* and the multiplication of trivia. Some of the huge bank of knowledge we've acquired over the past couple of hundred years of industrialisation can well be left alone, but the rest can be used in a different way from now.'

He agreed, but added: 'I think you've also got to tackle the next stage: that's to say, this alternative society should include the people who are making the materials for your heat pumps and all your other things. If you go on getting your materials by condemning people to the factory system and exploitation, you aren't achieving very much. But if they have the freedom to join you then there *is* an alternative society. Most of the examples I've seen are dependent on accumulated capital, which will sustain them for their first generation of equipment and materials, but when that runs out they won't be able to re-create their own. They'll either go down to a lower standard of living or depend on fresh input from the society which they've rejected. Remember, the things you need require very large inputs of high-energy density technology to manufacture – and you're going to depend on semi-heavy, if not heavy industry. You're picking the easy bit with the lowest capital demand. The scaling down of industrial processes to produce reasonable quality goods is difficult – it caused great distress and trouble to the Chinese when they tried to introduce it on a small scale. In the end they managed because they didn't know how difficult it was going to be – if they'd known in advance they probably wouldn't have done so.

'Of course, if you decide to go back to a mediaeval type of society, relying on blacksmiths' equipment, animal power and the rest of it, that's an energy level much easier to achieve and you're not dependent on outside people of this sort. The Chinese commune is the nearest working model to your relatively rural society that I'm likely to see in my lifetime.'

He believed that the biosphere could tolerate thermally the amount of energy the world was using at present. There were two problems: one was sharing it equably instead of unfairly as now; the other was finding abundant sources of extra energy that are cheap, easy to handle, safe, and clean. This was where equilibrium technology came in. It was not to be confused with *survival* technology, he stressed. 'That's merely what's needed to maintain the lowest grade of steady state you can think of – where you're entirely dependent on your own resources, using simple metals and other materials. We certainly don't want to go to *that* level –

its cultural and intellectual life is far too low and the population you could sustain would be absolutely minimal. You're not looking for that and neither am I, but somehow you've got to scale down your industrial processes, minimise the use of energy, get processes that minimise pollution and are more equable for people working in industry.

'As the Chinese have shown, this scaling down of industry is possible, but it's where we've had little experience. Scaling *up* represents a hundred years of industrial activity – all our training has been directed towards this growth pattern – like economic growth, it's the field of maximum endeavour. Scaling down requires research, but in your alternative society you can't provide the input to provide the research facilities and everything else. So in the end you can't opt out of present society except by going back to the survival level. I think the danger is that you might give people a complacent idea that by taking their savings out of the Post Office Savings Bank they can go and get into a community that is ecologically jolly good and will keep them in the standards to which they've been generally accustomed.'

Everyone in the rich societies had to be made to realise that maintaining these standards was no longer possible because the rest of the world were wanting to catch up – they felt they had a right to use a similar amount of energy. So the demonstration effect of intentional communities should not be wholly for the developed world, but at a level of a demand for energy and resources which the rest of the world could also expect. 'But,' he cautioned, 'I don't think your efforts will be understandable to most of the poor of the Third World – they want to move on to a different sort of society.'

Harold Dickinson was clearly thinking chiefly of survivalists within the academic world when he stressed that most of the people involved in the problem which we had been discussing had to work in real society with their own or other people. 'Then whenever there's a hiatus and people don't know what to do, we are there as the ones who *do* know what the next step is to bring society nearer to an equilibrium technology.

'You can't opt out. It's got to be a *political* act as well as a social and technological act to make any change in our society. Opting out – in the sense of the individual leaving it – is a drain which we can't afford in terms of numbers because there's too few of us already trying to make these fundamental changes.'

Chapter Nine:
Working for the revolution tomorrow

In the spectacular countryside of Kirkcudbrightshire, one group of people is attempting political action to achieve change, while demonstrating that communal life does work. It is Laurieston Hall, where ten adults and eight children live in a 65-room ex-stately home set in 12 once-sedate acres. Now the long corridors of the house are bare except for heaps of tools, equipment, cartons, and firewood; the décor of the rooms occupied by the communards ranges from disorderly to exotic, and the visitors' bedrooms boast little more than mattresses on bare floors.

The group which set up the commune comprised two archi-tects, a management consultant, an advertising agency executive, an interior designer, a computer systems analyst, a civil engineer, two teachers and a medical laboratory technician – in all, four women, six men and eight children, basically the same group as when I stayed there. It began with the familiar mixture of disenchantment with the imposed society and a yearning for peace in a rural setting, and moved steadily towards becoming a 'People Centre'. This orientation grew partly from the views held by the group, partly from the sheer size of the Hall. They had never envisaged anything so huge, but paradoxically they found during their long search for a place that anything smaller cost more.. After a hasty debate, they sold their city homes, bought Laurieston Hall, and in 1972 moved in.

When I stayed there a year later I experienced something of the acute problem of dividing time and energy among repairing a dilapidated mansion, getting together as a group, establishing a one-and-a-half-acre organic vegetable garden, learning to keep livestock, running a hostel, debating their aims and putting them into practice. At the end of my stay, the experience left me with even more than the usual sense of disorientation and elation which accompanies the transition from 'alternative' to 'straight' society.

The 'People Centre' as it has evolved has three main activities. An experiment in covering aspects of political, sociological, and environmental subjects not accorded status by universities came into being in the summer of 1974 and was called the 'Alternative University', for want of a better name. It attracted some 250 people throughout its six-week term.

A Community Project, in which children from depressed inner-city areas stay for short periods, grew in an *ad hoc* way, and evoked a response from community workers that took the three sponsoring members by surprise. The 'Kids Project', as it became called, offered not only a holiday in the country, but an accepting atmosphere for children found 'unacceptable' at home, by the courts, and in conventional corrective hostels. The sponsors running it had all worked in urban community projects and they wanted to build trustworthy relationships in an atmosphere of responsible freedom. Most of the children who came have come back for more.

The third activity, Women's Liberation, developed to become a strong link between the Hall and the outside community, and also involves long-stay visitors to the commune. Regular weekly meetings are held, members go to the national conferences of the Movement and maintain contact with women in other communities. In addition, spontaneous meetings are held during the 'Alternative University'.

But Laurieston Hall is not just a venue for conferences and meetings or a kids' holiday camp. It is firstly the home of the five family groups who live there; it is also a place to which people – singly or in groups – go to live for weeks or months and then move on; and it is a place where others, not on any particular business, stay for a few days. As one of the members explained to me later: 'To me a great deal of what Laurieston "is" is the immediate and all-involving interaction with the people here, either permanent or visiting – it's hard to make a clear distinction between the two. We all feel it, and no doubt it explains the "high" feeling you mentioned when you left; something others have also experienced, and that we *also* feel after groups or individuals leave.'

If I were to search for a word to describe this atmosphere it would probably be 'trust'. It is central to the whole community. There is no 'pocket money': any member can write a cheque or dip into the petty cash, merely writing the amount and its purpose in a book for all to see. To earn the Hall's £7,000 a year upkeep needs, some members go out to work. There is no compulsion about this; the need is discussed and a solution as to who goes and who stays is talked through. Neither is there any compulsion about chores: volunteers write their names on a board for cooking, cleaning and other duties. If anyone fails to volunteer enough, someone is sure to notice and, again, the problem – if there is one – is talked through.

But life at Laurieston is not yet Utopia, as another member reminded me: 'At the top of the stair near my room the metal banister has come loose. It's been held in place now since I don't know when by a piece of wood jammed in at chest height, and dozens of people carrying babies, armfuls of clothes, trays of food, mattresses and blankets and chairs, have ducked under it thousands of times. Sometimes, bent down by weights and worries, I've cracked my head on it. We've written a notice on the piece of wood to draw people's attention to it so they won't bang into it. Maybe tomorrow I'll mix up some concrete and mend it.' And he went on to say that they keep bees but lose more than they keep; their children prefer processed food to wholesome 'organic'; the goats had ingrowing toenails and not enough to eat; that some members felt that looking after the animals and garden was a non-productive pastime doing nothing to hasten 'the revolution'; and in any case if they didn't laboriously import tons of material from outside their 12 acres, the organic garden would simply produce less and less. 'But,' he added, 'a lot of people come here and have a great time.'

Towards Utopia

Divided, fluid, impecunious, inexperienced, outnumbered, yet dynamic, exhilarating and inspiring – Laurieston Hall resembles the Alternative in miniature: disparate people united chiefly by their common humanity and their commitment to changing the imposed society. For the Alternative recognises that, however alienating life within the affluent industrial nation may be, the materialism and living standards which make it endurable are bought at the expense of the poor of the Third World, the health of the biosphere, and the survival of children born today.

They know too well that the *status quo* is not easily budged. An alternative society threatens not only the empires of business and bureaucracy but living standards – both actual and desired – of workers in affluent countries and the Third World alike. Change is easily presented as a plot to prevent others achieving what a bunch of bored élitists has grown tired of. This being so, if the system which spawned and now supports the *status quo* of industrialisation were not showing signs of imminent collapse and failing to deliver the promised goodies, the prospects for survival would be grim indeed. For although much of the mis- guided technology which has made the whole monstrous edifice possible has been due to the discoveries of non-neutral scientists, technology has, in the past generally, responded to what people have asked for – however misguided, conditioned, and subjected to propaganda they may have grown.

So long as the energy to produce goods and live comfortably can still be bought, so long as cities still function – however creakingly – most people will opt for the *status quo*. But that does not stamp any seal of guarantee for the future. The *status quo* in cities is under fire from determined dissenters. Therein lies hope, for history has repeatedly shown that the strength of a *moral* force does not depend on numbers.

The author Ethel Mannin stressed this in *Bread and Roses*.

'The change of heart requisite for the realisation of millennium is not, ultimately, a matter of conversion from one idea to another, but of the collapse – from exhaustion – of existing systems. Civilisations rise and fall; the machine accelerates to the point at which it blows itself up . . . There are tides in the affairs of men that wash away systems and civilisations. And the tide is rising in the world today, though few realise it, and Nature herself is taking a hand in the process. The Earth, the source of all life, is losing its fertility; Nature is being revenged for the profligacy of Man . . . *Man must find a new way of living or perish* . . . the values of our civilisation are the urban values of the stock exchange and the market-place, and therefore none of the steps in the right direction advocated by the Planners, and reformers in general, can be anything but continual readjustments in a losing struggle for survival – the makeshifts by which a system fundamentally anti-life is kept going.'

When Ethel Mannin wrote these words 30 years ago, she made it clear that people should not wait passively for imperialist governments to experience a change of heart. And they are not! Today, as we have seen, awareness is spreading and action is growing. Misapplied technology is being recognised as a major force for exploitation, but the belief that a mere switch to an alternative technology alone would in itself create the necessary change is now seen as naïve. Political change is also needed. As Mike Reid, of Laurieston Hall, pointed out during a debate I attended there: 'Capitalism can absorb any AT hardware and turn it into a profitable commodity. General Motors can make windmills at popular prices; *Playboy* can advertise jock-straps made from soya beans; Chairs of Biotechnics can be endowed in all the best universities, and knighthoods awarded to designers of eco-office blocks.' Without politics, AT becomes nothing more than a set of trendy technical fixes.

None of the established political parties offers any hope – in Britain, or any other industrial nation. In the USA it was the recognition of this that brought about the Movement for A New Society which we encountered in Chapter One. The MNS set up a network of autonomous groups across the country, all committed to radical social change. They got together and produced a detailed analysis of the present system, and developed a vision of a better one. They trained their members to lead a sustained non-violent struggle to build a sense of community and alternative institutions. Corporate capitalism and the military machine were identified as the major culprits of the present system: underprivileged people and the planet the inevitable victims.

I talked with several of the youthful, energetic members of MNS in Philadelphia, one of them, George Lakey, author of *Strategy for a Living Revolution* There he outlined the several stages of a strategy born from his experience of activism with MNS and other groups in Britain and America. The first stage was one well recognised by revolutionaries in South America, where it has been given the name 'conscientisation' – an awareness by people that their private problems are, in truth, *political* issues. This stage prepares them for revolution – cultural preparation, he termed it. This was the time for strongly motivated agitators to speak on street corners, distribute leaflets, publish news sheets, and form study groups to explain the connection between the citizen and the system and paint a picture of an alternative society. He stressed the importance of street speaking – how it developed fluency, brought the agitator face to face with people and countered élitist tendencies. As he explained in his book, at the next stage the agitators become organisers to help people confront the *status quo*. Revolutionaries were to be found in tight-knit conspiratorial groups, in progressive community associations and communes – the alternatively based institutions I described in Chapter Five – in student organisations, labour unions, and the radical caucuses of professional associations – such as social workers, scientists, teachers, architects. All work openly, not underground.

In the third stage deeds supersede words: demonstrators fraternise with police and soldiers to help them see their viewpoint; reactionary institutions are boycotted; non-cooperation on the economic and political front is fomented. This leads to the fourth stage of mass non-cooperation: boycotting consumer goods, refusing to pay taxes, striking for worker control and so on, until the courts become clogged and 'It becomes a badge of honour to suffer for the revolution.' Finally, small teams of three to a dozen are encouraged to grow as cells grow, by division – in the way that the MNS has grown. These teams – Groups of Living Revolution – help the waiting counter-institutions to become the new institutions of the people; while the radical professional caucuses occupy and control the organisations of local and national life. Coordinating councils work at every level for a smooth transfer of power from corporations and government to the people's institutions.

It is possible, as George Lakey has done, to suggest a strategy. No revolution can succeed by imposition, however – the will for change must stem from the people. They must be helped to become more aware of their relationship with the real world beyond their private lives, and of their potential to become effective in it. Whether a revolution in attitudes can be won by a predetermined strategy, or whether it will rise naturally – as Ethel Mannin paints, 'like a tide' – two vital instruments for change exist and their potential must not be ignored: they are firstly education and secondly the communication media of press, television, and radio.

Little help can be expected from the huge institution of formal schooling that is part of the imposed society and harnessed to serve it. Fortunately, this institution is already the subject of deep questioning, and the search for alternatives is happening both within its establishment and outside it. As the crisis in society deepens, the role of education can be expected to change: from producing 'factory fodder' and conditioned consumers, to creating questioners, eager to participate in the quest for survival within a more humane society.

Similarly, little help can be expected from the existing mass communications media, the majority firmly controlled by the system and dependent – chiefly through advertising revenue – upon its continuance as a consumer society. We have seen, in

Chapter Five, however, that new, small-scale media devoted to change are coming into being, and the book's Source Guide lists a number of them. They may be expected to grow. They range through community television and radio stations; community, national and transnational news-letters, newspapers, magazines, books and catalogues; information services; travelling vans equipped with film and video tape projectors and exhibition material; study groups, seminars, festivals – and plain word of mouth.

Indiana Farm Boy
Alternative media cover a wide spectrum of ideology and activity, but almost without exception they have one thing in common: each sprang from the dedication of one or two people, usually without funds, written or filmed and put together by unpaid volunteers in somebody's home and somehow got out to its audience in spite of establishment distribution agencies. Just outside Hendersonville in North Carolina I spoke with Jane and John Shuttleworth who, in 1969, put together the first issue of their magazine on the kitchen table, and now run what is possibly the most powerful medium for change in the whole alternative movement.

The Mother Earth News comes out bi-monthly, a magazine which John calls 'a serialised survival manual for the future'. Like its founder, it has a strongly practical personality. In every issue articles on alternative energy and organic food-growing predominate; people who have exchanged city life for remote farms or rural communes tell their stories; several pages carry names and addresses of people with farms and those who want to work on them; articles on the horrors of nuclear power brush with features on goat-keeping and jam-making. The whole has a friendly, folksy tone as if writers and readers were all one family. *The Mother Earth News* is a thoroughly professional publishing production smacking of commercialism, and yet it contrives to carry with it the wholesomeness of the country, the ingenuity of scrap technology, and the urgency of the ecological crisis told with missionary fervour. To the ultra-sophisticated it is some kind of bad joke; to the idealist it is a means to turn a dream into reality; and to the cynic it is an enviable way to make a publishing buck out of the ecological crisis plus the well-heeled city dweller's urge to escape it. For today, the readers of *Mother* – as its devotees call it – number hundreds of thousands; a sister bimonthly, *Lifestyle*, has been launched; the organisation includes book publishing and mail order; and plans are well advanced for a multi-million-dollar non-profit research station into self-sufficiency – the last-named seen by triumphant critics as a normal guilt-ridding adjunct to just another success story.

'I'm no seer,' John insisted from the outset, 'I'm just an Indiana farm boy. I grew up on one of the poorest farms in the county, and – built up by organic methods – it's now one of the best, while others on a heavy chemical trip have gone downhill.' He explained that he had left the farm to gain experience and had done just about every kind of job, and this showed him how people could live outside the system. 'At the end of the sixties, Jane and I were making money we didn't need, to buy things we didn't want, doing jobs we didn't like, to impress people we didn't even care for. We decided "To hell with it, let's drop out, get a little farm." But we realised you can't live alone as free people in a closed society, so we said, "Let's try to help set others free at the same time." So we began *The Mother Earth News*.'

They had meagre resources; the 'office' was their home; they often worked 18 hours a day: but they were helped by young people who came and worked for nothing, sometimes living with them. It was a long haul, but eventually the magazine began to grow. I asked him why. 'When we started, our basic philosophy was to give more than we could ever expect to get in return. But if you're taught to operate the way we're taught in the United States which is "me first", you pull against what I believe to be a "life force", and life becomes very difficult. You may be successful, but you become embittered. If instead you give more than you have to give, you create a vacuum – and that "life force" comes rushing in so fast it gives you more than you deserved in the first place.'

'But you must have had some policy, a strategy. . . .'

'Our model was not to overthrow the establishment but to "underwhelm" it: insidiously seep into the cracks in their minds and turn their heads around. We were going to fight a guerrilla warfare with the establishment and we needed weapons: dollars were our rifles. We said we were going to get hold of some of those dollars and start doing a good thing for people – to help them realise their dreams – for that's what Utopia is all about. We learned to use the marketing methods of the system. Now we say to our readers, "Hey man, you're going to be a sexier stud – not by using our toothpaste, but by reading our magazine – you'll save a lot of money." We use all the old advertising tricks. We believe that people will start living differently out of self-interest, enjoy it *and* find it's kinder to the planet too. We're trying to set people free one by one, a family here, a commune there – to help them get together and get organised.'

I asked him the question about people who couldn't get out of the cities, and he came back smartly: 'We never said "Everybody off to the land" – that's why we've started *Lifestyle* – to help people in cities live differently, to survive. For this to happen we've got to re-organise society completely and get away from raping the countryside to support the cities. We've got to get back to the "village" way of organising society where every individual area is basically self-contained – so that someone can *walk* to get everything he needs. In this country you can't – you have to get into an automobile. It's dumb! We've become slaves to our machines. The change is going to take a few generations: here we're just trying to lay the groundwork.'

He told me he still worked seven days a week and paid himself 136 dollars a week; every nickel he possessed was in the business and he still owed his relatives for the money they put in to get it started; he and Jane lived simply – they had one second-hand truck which was shared with the business. I asked what drove him to live this way.

'I have a particular talent to write the kind of articles we specialise in and I can help others to do the same. I'm working myself to death doing it. It's ridiculous, but I do it. Time is running out. The planet has to come first. We are stewards of the Earth – that's our foremost obligation. And we have failed miserably. When I see how we've raped and pillaged this country in the name of progress, it reminds me of an old gospel song, "I don't feel at home in this world any more". We're like a bunch of savages: we've exchanged our birthright for chrome automobiles and little boxes which give you colour pictures of a bunch of drivel. We're steadily decreasing the planet's resources and increasing our demands on them. There's going to be pestilence, plagues, wars – everything you can think of. Here at *The Mother Earth News* we're just little people trying to do a big job. I'll do anything to reach people with the idea that there *are* alternatives, that we do have to change, and that to get from point A to point B we have to start right now.'

Before I left Hendersonville, I checked: pretty well everything he had told me was verified. He did work as hard as he said: the proposed research station was no status symbol but an intention to pioneer work in an essential but neglected field. And to the chagrin of the lurking cynics, any findings would *not* be exclusive to *Mother* and *Lifestyle*.

An Alternative to Recapitulation

It is a convention that the closing passages of a book should wrap up its theme in a neat package, after the fashion of the encapsulated, pre-digested half-hour TV documentary. I shall not do this: I would too easily fall into the trap of 'blueprintism'. As much as can be said of my journey has been said, and the reader – if he is so motivated – must himself work to draw his own conclusions from the opinions and actions of the people I have met, accepting or rejecting them – as he will no doubt also judge my own interspersed observations. Having said that, I still feel compelled to add a few closing thoughts.

In writing this book, I have had Britain in mind, for it is *my place* – of my beginning and probably my ending. Why then so much about The United States? I make no apology. Firstly, I had to go there to learn what the Alternative was thinking and doing, and relate it to Britain and the rest of the world. Secondly, no other people in history have destroyed so much of the planet – both on their home ground and from the resources they have imported – in so short a time, and with such dramatic and tragic consequences. No other nation has accumulated so much material wealth from exploiting people and planet alike, nor distributed it so unevenly. The central conflict between satisfying the insatible wants of a minority of mankind and satisfying the needs of the biosphere is nowhere more sharply drawn. Action on such a grand scale could be expected to generate a comparably prodigious reaction: the experience of my travels there – which coincided with the dual traumas of energy deprivation and political turmoil – confirmed that this is indeed happening. The United States, therefore, offers the rest of the world not only an awful lesson, but the hope of a solution. The American encounters I have described have both a direct and indirect relevance to the rest of the world – both overdeveloped and underdeveloped.

Keeping the American experience in mind, I would wish to leave the reader with confirmation of the view – no longer original – that the urban-industrial society which a minority of the world has embraced, and which has become a model for the élite of the rest of the world to imitate, cannot be sustained except at the expense of today's underprivileged and of future generations – indeed at the risk of despatching the kind of planet we inhabit. The survivalists in their disparate ways are working towards a different scenario of the future, believing one to be possible. It *is* possible, but only when an alternative way of living becomes acceptable – one which is obviously more satisfying and desirable than the imposed way. It is because I have hope for this *grassroots* origin of future change rather than another *imposed* solution that I saved John Shuttleworth's earthy comments until last. If change is to happen, it must begin with each one of us. To utter pious hopes while continuing to consume excessively and remain part of the machinery of excessive consumption must be seen to be untenable.

This book abounds with ideas on how anyone – with or without money – can work towards creating an alternative society. As I have said, it is not necessary to grow a beard or eat brown rice, and it is certainly not desirable that the inexperienced should rush out to the land and try to husband it. Plenty of work needs to be done: firstly upon ourselves, and secondly upon the institutions to which each of us belongs. The aim of this book – if it has one – has been to reveal the opportunities and the options that are open. A Source Guide gives the names and addresses of groups who will gladly take the revelation further.

Finally, an appeal. If change does spread, the days of the consumer society with its dependency on monopoly capitalism, jobs, and centralised authority are numbered. Transition to a society based on new values will not be accomplished without pain and discomfort – though hopefully with far less violence than the maintenance of the present one insidiously inflicts each and every day. The energies of society's leading figures – in Parliament, in unions, in universities, in industry and beyond – would, I submit, be more humanely and sensibly employed studying the towering problems of transition than in straining for either personal gain or the wider goal of economic growth. Failure of the society which they helped to impose will indicate that they may need assistance. The survivalists, who are already humbly paving the way to a new one, will be happy to give all the assistance they can.

Epilogue

The book is finished but the journey continues. Even before the beginning of it, we knew – Shirley and I – that we could not continue to live as we had. We could no longer feel comfortable in a city, living well, while so many live with too little. Our way is to return to the country, for we have farmed before and we care for the land. The cottage we shall live in was falling down, and we are restoring it: with the insulation we are building in to it we should be warm on two or three kilowatts; hopefully some modest ideas for using alternative technology will come to fruition. Whatever happens, our demands will be small. Although we have shed many possessions we still have too many for comfort, but, as they wear out or break, few will be replaced. Our few acres are neglected – we shall husband them carefully to grow food for ourselves and, in time, for others. We hope to become part of a community. And we intend to spread the idea of change. To us there is nothing sacrificial in all this, for we know we are among the lucky ones. What we are doing is for our own peace and satisfaction: it is not an unselfish act. We shall be criticised, but this is our way. We have few illusions left. If we should be happy in what we do, it will be less at the expense of others, we shall have reduced our harm to the environment, and we may even have contributed a little. To continue the journey is better than standing by, watching.

Source Guide

On these pages, anyone who wants to read more or join something will find a selection of journals (also some "catalogue" type source guides) and a number of organizations. I've included subscription rates of the journals—p.a. indicates the annual rate—and membership fees of organizations where possible, though the Imposed Society's inevitable inflation may make some of them out of date by the time you read this. Reduced rates for students, unemployed prisoners and so on are often available, so if you think you qualify, it's worth mentioning. The asterisk against some of the organizations means they accept ordinary people as members; the others either want you to have special qualifications, or else they're not the kind that has a membership.

Several of the entries are mentioned in the text, so cross-check with the index and you might learn more. The entries here are simply the ones I've encountered that cover what the book is about. No doubt thousands which should be mentioned are not. To those who feel grieved about this, I say "I'm sorry." But there are enough here to help you find your way in—and once in you'll soon encounter more.

Reading Materials

ALTERNATIVE ENGLAND & WALES (U.K.)
Directory-size guide to just about every aspect of the alternative scene. Written and published by Nicholas Saunders, 1975, £2.50. Also ALTERNATIVE LONDON, published by Nicholas Saunders & Wildwood House, 29 King St., London WC2, 1973, 85p.
ALTERNATIVE SOCIETY (Canada)
Articles and news about the Canadian commune movement. Monthly. North Star Tribe, 10 Thomas St., St. Catherine's, Ont.
ALTERNATIVE SOURCES OF ENERGY (U.S.)
Alternative technologies for a decentralized society. Hard information

plus reviews, letters, contact lists and reports of meetings. Quarterly, $5.00 p.a. $6.00 elsewhere. Rt.2, Box 90-A, Milaca, Minn. 56353.

ALTERNATIVES (U.S.)
Publish Alternate Celebration Catalogue plus a newsletter. Their motto is "Working for simpler lifestyles through alternate celebrations." P.O Box 20626, Greensboro, N.C. 27420.

APPROPRIATE TECHNOLOGY (U.K.)
Third World oriented, newsy and practical. Quarterly, £3.50 p.a. Intermediate Technology Development Group, 9 King St., London WC2.

ARCHITECTURAL DESIGN (U.K.)
Alternative technology among daunting, "straight" architecture. Monthly. £8.40 p.a. 26 Bloomsbury Way, London WC1.

CLOUDBURST (Canada)
A Handbook of Rural Skills and Technology. Cloudburst Press, Box 79, Brackendale, B.C.

COEVOLUTION QUARTERLY (U.S.)
Continues in depth the concepts of the WHOLE EARTH CATALOG & EPILOG. 144 pages, color cover, illustrations, no advertising. $8.00 p.a. Single issue, $2.50. Box 428, Sausalito, Calif. 94965.

COMMUNITY PUBLICATIONS COOPERATIVE (U.S.)
Booklist of resources on community/cooperative living and working. Both theoretical and practical works available. Free catalogue. Box 426, Louisa, Va. 23093.

DEVELOPMENT NEWS DIGEST (Australia)
A forum for a wide cross-section of opinion on development issues. Encourages a critical and questioning approach. Five times a year, A$3.00. Published by the Education Unit of the Australian Council for Overseas Aid, P.O. Box 1562, Canberra City, A.C.T. 2601.

DIRECTORY OF ALTERNATIVE WORK (U.K.)
Lists self-management and radical technology projects that have got off the ground. Uncareers, 298b Pershore Road, Birmingham 5.

HENRY DOUBLEDAY RESEARCH ASSOCIATION NEWS-LETTER (U.K.)
Readable reports of experiments at the Association's own trial grounds and in members' gardens. A "must" for organic growers. 20 Convent Lane, Bocking, Braintree, Essex.

EARTH GARDEN (Australia)
Concerned with non-polluted living and growing, the back-to-the-land movement, surviving in the city and the bush, food and diet, and the inner changes which follow when you are in tune with Nature. Nos. 1-11 A$11.00 Nos. 11-14 A$5.00. P.O. Box 111, Balmain, Vic. 2041.

THE ECOLOGIST (U.K.)
Journal of the post-industrial age. Small-scale and technical alternatives and analyses of mankind's disaster course. Monthly. £5.50 p.a. (U.S. $12.00.) Gatesby, Molesworth Street, Wadebridge, Cornwall.

ECOLOGY LAW QUARTERLY (U.S.)
Devoted to legal planning and policy issues in environmental affairs. Considers such issues as energy use, urban growth control, food shortages, economic policy, and international commerce. Cross-disciplinary research for activists, lawyers, scientists, legislators, businessmen. $12.00 p.a. Boalt Hall, School of Law, University of California, Berkeley, Calif. 94720.

GRASS ROOTS (Australia)
Craft and lifestyle magazine for those who wish to regain control over their lifestyle by exploring the alternatives to modern mass consumption. Country bias. A$4.00 for 4 issues. Box 900, Shepparton, Vic.

THE GREEN REVOLUTION (U.S.)
Newsletter of the School of Living. Devoted to the back-to-the-land movement. $4.00 p.a. Route 1, Box 129, Freeland, Md. 21053.

IN THE MAKING (U.K.)
An annual directory of proposed projects in self-management and radical technology. 50p, including two or three supplements in between. 221 Albert Road, Sheffield 8, Yorks.

JOURNAL OF THE NEW ALCHEMISTS (U.S.)
Straight research papers on biotechnics and organic food production plus lighter stuff. Normally only available through associate membership of the Institute, $25.00. P.O Box 432, Woods Hole, Mass. 02543.

THE MOTHER EARTH NEWS (U.S.)
More than a magazine . . . a way of life. Practical articles mixed with homespun philosophy. Stresses alternative lifestyles, ecology, working with nature and doing more with less. Bi-monthly. $10.00 p.a. ($12.00 outside U.S.). P.O. Box 70, Hendersonville, N.C. 28739.

NEW ENGLAND SOLAR ENERGY NEWSLETTER (U.S.)
A monthly report on developments in solar, wind, and wood energy, slanted toward readers with practical applications in mind. Published by the New England Chapter of the American Section of the International Solar Energy Society, P.O. Box 121, Townshend, Vt. 05353.

THE NEW INTERNATIONALIST
A magazine about the people, the ideas and the action in the fight for world development. (U.K.) £4.75 p.a. R.P.S. Ltd., Victoria Hall, Fingal St., London SE10. (U.S.) $15.00. New World Coalition, Room 209, 409 Boylston St., Boston, Mass. 02116. (Canada) $12.00. P.O. Box 3460, Halifax, Nova Scotia B3J 2J1.

NORTH AMERICAN SURVIVAL AND HOMESTEADING AS-
SOCIATION (Canada)
Sells and lends a large assortment of materials on self-sufficiency.
Catalogue with hundreds of listings for 25⊄ Box 4077, Station A, Toronto,
Ont. M5W 1M4.

NOT MAN APART (U.S.)
Updates on major environmental action, some international news, information for citizen action. Newspaper published twice monthly. $10.00
p.a. Friends of the Earth, 529 Commercial St., San Francisco, Calif.
94111.

NUTRITION ACTION (U.S.)
Research and news about food and food actions across the United States.
$10.00 p.a. Center for Science in the Public Interest, 1779 Church St.,
N.W., Washington, D.C. 20036. Also publish PEOPLE & ENERGY
monthly newletter devoted to citizen action in nuclear power. $7.50 p.a.

ORGANIC GARDENING AND FARMING (U.S.)
Practical and theoretical articles. 33 East Minor St., Emmaus, Pa.,
18049. Also publish COMPOST SCIENCE.

PLANETARY CITIZENS (U.S.)
Works to enlist people (mainly prominent) throughout the world as
"planetary citizens." Membership and subscription to quarterly newsletter, ONE FAMILY, $5.00 p.a. 777 United Nations Plaza, New York,
N.Y. 10017.

THE POWDER MAGAZINE (Australia)
A radical source guide to liberation (national, women's, gay), anti-racism,
deschooling and alternative technology, published by The Light, Powder
and Construction Company, an information center concerned with the
relationship between Western industrialized Society and the Third World.
Monthly (approx.) A$5.00 p.a. P.O. Box 18060, GPO, Melbourne, Vic.
3001.

PRACTICAL SELF-SUFFICIENCY (U.K.)
Aims to fulfill its title. £3.50 for six issues in U.K., £5.00 elsewhere.
Broad Leys Publishing Co., Widdington, Saffron Walden, Essex CB11
3SP.

RADICAL TECHNOLOGY
Directory-size, 304-page guide to food, shelter, tools, materials, energy,
communications, autonomy, and community. (U.K.) £3.25. Wildwood
House. 29 King St., London WC2. (U.S.) $5.95. Pantheon Books, 201
East 50th St., New York, N.Y. 10022.

RESURGENCE (U.K.)
Journal of the Fourth World; seeks answers to global problems of war,
militarism, industrialism, pollution, and alienation; asserts they can be

solved only if political and economic units are made small, technology simple and our mode of living organic—hence the Fourth World of decentralized, small-scale, non-materialistic forms of organization. Bi-monthly. (U.K.) £3.40 p.a. Elsewhere $10.00 (air $15.00). Eastbourne House, Bullards Place, London E2.

SCIENCE FOR THE PEOPLE (U.S.)
Journal of the organization, SESPA. Bi-monthly $12.00 (or what you can afford). 9 Walden St., Jamaica Plain, Mass. 02130.

SHELTER (U.S.)
Lavishly illustrated "catalogue"-type book of simple and beautiful dwellings, natural materials, and human resourcefulness. Also about freedom, self-discovery, self-sufficiency, and survival. $6.00. Shelter Publications, P.O. Box 279, Bolinas, Calif. 94924. (U.S. and Canada distributors, Random House.)

SHELTER SOURCE BOOK (U.S.)
Describes responsibly designed products available in many fields. Chapters include: Enclosure, Energy, Water and Waste, Lighting, Food and Greenhouses, Communication, Transportation, Furniture, and Clothing. Edited by Nicholas Peckham. $4.50. Planet Press, 1500 East Walnut St., Columbia, Mo. 65201.

SIERRA CLUB BULLETIN (U.S.)
Monthly magazine dedicated to restoring the quality of the natural environment and maintaining the integrity of ecosystems. Lists activities including programs to "study, explore, and enjoy wildlands." $8.00 p.a. Sierra Club, 530 Bush St., San Francisco, Calif. 94108.

THE SOIL ASSOCIATION (U.K.)
Articles on growing food organically and on health generally. Monthly. (See Soil Association entry for address.)

SPARK (U.S.)
Semi-annual journal directed toward institutionalized engineering. Published by The Committee for Social Responsibility in Engineering, 475 Riverside Drive, New York, N.Y. 10027.

SURVIVAL SCRAPBOOKS (U.K.)
A series of six finely illustrated introductory guides to shelter, food, energy, tools, etc. with extensive bibliographies. About £1.50 each. Stefan Szczelkun, Unicorn Books, Nant Gwilw, Llanfynnydd, Carmarthen, Wales

UNDERCURRENTS (U.K.)
Bi-monthly magazine of radical science and people's technology: politcal rhetoric mixed in with windmills and the rest. (U.K. £2.50 p.a. (U.S.) $7.50. Earth Exchange Building, 213 Archway Road, London N6 5BN.

WHOLE EARTH CATALOG (U.S.)
Unsurpassed for coverage and honesty as a basic access tool on self-sufficiency and AT—that is, until its 1974 successor, WHOLE EARTH EPILOG. CATALOG $6.00. EPILOG $4.00. (U.S. distributors, Penguin Books, 625 Madison Ave., New York, N.Y. 10017.)

WORKFORCE (U.S.)
Campaigns for all oppressed minorities in America and Third World. Seeks to change the system non-violently. Bi-monthly, published by Vocations for Social Change. (See separate entry.)

Organizations

ALTERNATIVE SOCIETY (U.K.) *
Aims to join together the fragments of an alternative society: business organization, education, politics, and community. Holds conferences and workshops.£2.00 p.a. 9 Moreton Ave. Kidlington, Oxford.

BIT (U.K.) *
An information service on every facet of alternative living with contacts throughout Europe. Coordinates CLAP (Community Levy for Alternative Projects) whereby successful ventures give financial support to new ones; also publishes an information digest with a different name each issue, £1.00 p.a. 146 Great Western Road, London, W11.

BRACE RESEARCH INSTITUTE (Canada)
Specializes in Third World problems, but its technical pamphlets have general application. List from them at: McDonald College, McGill University, St. Anne de Bellevue, 800 Quebec.

BRITISH SOCIETY FOR SOCIAL RESPONSIBILITY IN SCIENCE (BSSRS) (U.K.)*
Aims to alert scientists, engineers, and technologists to the social role of their work, and make the public aware of technology's developments and dangers. 9 Poland St., London W1V 3DG.

THE CTT ASSOCIATION (U.K.) *
Offspring of CONSERVATION TOOLS & TECHNOLOGY LTD. (formerly LOW IMPACT TECHNOLOGY LTD), a design and consultancy service in building and energy management, the Association publishes a quarterly newsletter, ALTERNATIVE ENERGY SOURCES, plus discounts on CTT products and publications—wind generators, solar collectors, water turbines, and so on, and publications on alternative energy sources and self-sufficiency. £5.40 p.a. individuals £27.00 educational, £54.00 corporate. 143 Maple Road, Surbiton, Surrey.

COMMITTEE FOR SOCIAL RESPONSIBILITY IN ENGINEERING (CSRE) (U.S.)
475 Riverside Drive, New York, N.Y. 10027.

THE CONSERVATION SOCIETY (U.K.)*
Britain's largest environmental pressure group. Began with population as its central issue, but now concerns itself with whole question of survival. Branches also champion specific local issues. £4.00 p.a. 12 London St., Chertsey, Surrey KT16 8AA.

HENRY DOUBLEDAY RESEARCH ASSOCIATION (U.K.) *
Aims to improve and encourage horticulture. Researches organic methods with members' help, making results widely known. Analyzes protein and vitamin content of fruit and vegetables. Promotes the high-yielding protein plant, comfrey. £3.00 includes quarterly newsletter. 20 Convent Lane, Bocking, Braintree, Essex.

ECOLOGY PARTY (U.K)
A political party with policies based on the principle that mankind must learn to live in harmony with nature within limits of the earth's finite supply of resources. 16 West Park Road, Leeds 8.

ENVIRONMENTAL ACTION REPRINT SERVICE (EARS) (U.S.)
A clearinghouse for information on nuclear energy, alternative sources of energy, and energy policy in the U.S. A wide variety of printed information and films available at low prices. 2239 East Colfax Ave., Denver, Colo. 80206.

FARM AND FOOD SOCIETY (U.K.)*
Promotes rational use of land through organic husbandry; believes in self-sufficiency in food for Britain. 37 Tanza Road, London NW3.

FOOD ACTION CENTER (U.S.)
A major focal point for food action on college campuses across the U.S. Publish FOOD ACTION EXCHANGE newsletter. 2115 S St., N.W., Washington, D.C. 20008.

FRIENDS OF THE EARTH*
Devoted to the preservation, restoration, and rational use of the earth. Oppose projects that offend the environment. 529 Commercial St., San Francisco, Calif. 94111.

INTERMEDIATE TECHNOLOGY DEVELOPMENT GROUP (ITDG) (U.K)
Specializes in Third World problems and publishes useful pamphlets, also journal. Parnell House, 25 Wilton Road, London, SW1. (U.S.) Peter Gillingham, 630 Magdalena Ave., Los Altos, Calif. 94022.

INTERNATIONAL SOLAR ENERGY SOCIETY
Interdisciplinary professional organization. Produces a quarterly journal (available to non-members) and a newsletter. (Australia) (Headquarters) Sec: W.R.W. Reid, P.O. Box 26, Highett, Vic. 3190. (U.S.) Sec: Dr. W.H. Klein, 12441 Parklawn Drive, Rockville, Md. 20852.

MOVEMENT FOR A NEW SOCIETY (U.S.)*
A network of small, autonomous groups working non-violently for a fundamental social change based on new values. Publish a newsletter called DANDELION. 1006 South 46th St., Phildelphia, Pa. 19143.

NEW ALCHEMY INSTITUTE (EAST) (U.S.)*
Pledged to "restore the lands, protect the seas, and inform the earth's stewards." Runs a decentralized research program with ordinary gardeners and others. List of excellent literature available on request. Associate membership $25.00 includes the Institute's journal. P.O. Box 432. Woods Hole, Mass. 02543.

NEW COMMUNITY PROJECT (U.S.)
Collective dedicated to developing lifestyle alternatives. Services include facilitation-consultation referral service, commune development, alternative family groups, workshops, speaker bureau, and research information. 302 Berkeley St., Boston, Mass. 02116.

THE NEW VILLAGES ASSOCIATION (UK.)*
Works to establish largely self-sufficient, land-based New Villages with populations around 1,000, and emphasis on lower consumption lifestyles. £1.00 p.a. 3 Salubrious, Broadway, Worcs. WR12 7AU.

SESPA SCIENCE FOR THE PEOPLE (U.S.)*
Works for social responsibility in science. 9 Walden St., Jamaica Plain, Mass. 02130.

THE SOIL ASSOCIATION (U.K.)*
Believes that organic husbandry best builds soil fertility, and produces the nourishing crops that improve human and animal health. Publishes monthly journal. £5.00 p.a. Walnut Tree Manor, Haughley, Stowmarket. Suffolk, 1P14 3RS.

VITA (Volunteers in Technical Assistance) (U.S.)
Provide solutions to Third World technical problems, usually through correspondence, and produce excellent publications, including Village Technology Handbook. ($9.00.) List from 3706 Rhode Island Ave., Mt. Rainier, Md. 20822.

VOCATIONS FOR SOCIAL CHANGE (U.S.)
A work collective spreading information about how people can gain control over their work situations and their own lives. Acts in solidarity with all who seek basic changes in the system imposed on them, but must stay where they are to effect change. Subsists on donations. Publishes bi-monthly journal, WORKFORCE. ($7.00 p.a.) 5951 Canning St., Oakland, Calif. 94609.

WORKING WEEKENDS ON ORGANIC FARMS (WWOOF) (U.K.)*
Experience of organic farming, food and lodging in exchange for work.
SAE to 143 Sabine Road, London SW11.

Bibliographical Notes

Chapter Two
Page 39 GEORGE M. WOODWELL, in *The Scientific American*, September 1970.
39 G. EVELYN HUTCHINSON, in *The Scientific American*, September 1970.
42 *Village One* (Village Design, Berkeley, 1972).
45 GORDON RATTRAY TAYLOR: *Re-think* (Dutton, 1972).
48 EDWARD HEATH, in *The Times*, 14 January 1974.
48 ANTHONY CROSLAND, in *The Ecologist*, March/ April 1974.
51 ROBIN CLARKE, in *New Scientist*, 11 January 1973.

Chapter Three
Page 58 *Energy and the Environment* (Institute of Fuel, Royal Society of Arts & Committee for Environmental Conservation, 1974).
60 ANTHONY TUCKER, in *The Guardian*, 15 April 1974.
64 *Newsletter of the Programme of Peace & Conflict Research* (University of Lancaster, Department of Politics, March 1974).
70 HANS W. HAMM, *Low Cost Development of Small Water-power Sites* (VITA: Volunteers for International Technical Assistance, New York).
74 RAM BUX SINGH, in *The Mother Earth News Handbook of Homemade Power* (Bantam Books, New York, 1974).

77 PHILIP BRACHI, in *The Ecologist*, February 1974.
78 PETER HARPER, in *Undercurrents*, No. 5, Winter 1973.

Chapter Four

Page 82 J. J. BURKE, in *The Times*, 16 January 1974.
83 TERENCE MCLAUGHLIN, in *Observer Magazine*, 12 May 1974.
90 *Greater London Council Housing Department Survey, 1968.*
91 S. V. SZOKOLAY, *An Experimental Solar House* (Polytechnic of Central London, Built Environment Research Group, March 1974).
92 *RSC Autonomous Housing Study – Dwelling Laboratory, Summary and Progress Report* (University of Cambridge, Technical Research Division, 18 December 1973).
95 STEVE BAER, in *The Mother Earth News*, No. 22, July, 1973.
103 JOHN O'CONNELL, in *The Sunday Times*, 5 May 1974.
104 B. HYDE & M. KIBBLEWHITE, *Building in Botswana* (University of Edinburgh, Science & Engineering, September 1973).

Chapter Five

Page 109 PETER HARPER, in *Impact of Science on Society*, Vol. XXIII, No. 4, 1973.
110 RADTECH-IN-PACT, in *Undercurrents*, No. 3, Autumn/Winter 1972.
112 *This is ICOM* (Industrial Common-Ownership Movement, 1974).
112 SCOTT BADER COMMONWEALTH, in *Small is Beautiful*, by E. F. Schumacher (Harper & Row, 1973).
113 TRYLON, in *Craft Teacher News*, September 1973.
114 BIT and COPE, in *Uncareers Alternative Work News Sheet*, July 1974.
116 KEITH HUDSON, in *Towards Survival*, No. 21, April 1974.

122   DES WILSON, in The Observer, 14 April 1974.
123   E. F. SCHUMACHER, in The Guardian, 10 April 1973.

Chapter Six
Page 138   PETER VAN DRESSER, A Landscape for Humans (Biotechnic Press, Albuquerque, 1972).
143   HAROLD DICKINSON, Rural China, 1972 (University of Edinburgh, School of Engineering Science, 1972).

Chapter Seven
Page 148   Preliminary Assessment of the World Food Situation Present and Future (United Nations, 1974).
150   LAWRENCE D. HILLS, Dig for Survival (Henry Doubleday Research Association).
151   PAUL HAWKEN on 'The Magic of Findhorn Gardens' in East West Journal, Boston.
154   JOHN JEAVONS, How to Grow More Vegetables than You ever Thought Possible on Less Land than You Can Imagine (Ecology Action of the Midpeninsular, Palo Alto, 1974).
163   HAROLD DICKINSON, Rural China, 1972 (University of Edinburgh, School of Engineering Science, 1972).

Chapter Eight
Page 180   National Centre for Alternative Technology and Resource Conservation, in Undercurrents, No. 8, October–November 1974.
Page 182   Newsletter of the Programme of Peace & Conflict Research (University of Lancaster, Department of Politics, March 1974).

Chapter Nine
Page 197   ETHEL MANNIN, Bread and Roses (MacDonald, 1944).
199   GEORGE LAKEY, Strategy for a Living Revolution (Grossman, New York, and W. H. Freeman, San Francisco, 1973).

Index